MARSHALL HOLMAN'S

BOWLING TIPS & TECHNIQUES

MARSHALL HOLMAN

WITH ROY G. NELSON

D0907944

CONTEMPORARY
BOOKS, INC.
CHICAGO

Library of Congress Cataloging-in-Publication Data

Holman, Marshall.
 Marshall Holman's Bowling tips and techniques

 Includes Index.
 1. Bowling.   I. Nelson, Roy G.   II. Title.
III. Title: Bowling tips and techniques
GV902.5.H64   1985   794.6   85-25453
ISBN 0-8092-5324-0

Published by Contemporary Books, Inc.
180 North Michigan Avenue, Chicago, Illinois 60601
Manufactured in the United States of America
Library of Congress Catalog Card Number: 85-25453
International Standard Book Number: 0-8092-5324-0

Published simultaneously in Canada by Beaverbooks, Ltd.
195 Allstate Parkway, Valleywood Business Park
Markham, Ontario L3R 4T8 Canada

CONTENTS

To my friends Jerome Lee and Andy Anderson with my deepest affection and gratitude.—**Marshall Holman**

To our Heavenly Father who through our Lord and Savior Jesus Christ has blessed me with the ability to write this book.—**Roy G. Nelson**

ACKNOWLEDGMENTS

Our special thanks to the Showboat Lanes and Hotel (Las Vegas, Nevada) for the use of their facility in photographing this book.

Also, our thanks to typists Bev Nelson and Marianne Foti; to Ralph Cohen, our editorialist; and to Rosemarie Nelson for her inspiration and help in assembling the text.

INTRODUCTION

As the lights hit the surface of the wooden lanes, the resilient finish seems to sparkle as though the lanes had just been bathed.

The announcers speak in muffled tones to a television and radio audience.

The bowler stands silhouetted on the lanes as he addresses his challenge, for stretched some 60 feet beyond are the objects of his attention—a triangular formation of 10 pins that has served as a target for generations.

In his hands he holds the means to their temporary destruction.

The tension mounts as the stage is set, and a hushed audience sits perched atop its bleacher seats, held in silent awe.

The drama and suspense that surround the moment seem to follow the plot of a Hollywood script; the tension in the air can be cut with a knife. The electricity in the atmosphere winds a mystical pattern that unknowingly seals a common bond among those in attendance.

For standing before our eyes, in this classic confrontation, is one of the most competitive athletes in all sports.

For many it's a dream, and for a select few a reality; for the athlete we see has attained the distinction of being called a "professional bowler!"

As his forward movement starts, so does that of the spectators, who now occupy the edge of their seats; with this movement the tension heightens, as he walks, then glides, toward the line in picturesque style.

It's as though he conducts a symphony through his effortless grace, with the music following his every pace. As he releases his ball, its path is strong and true, and he poses, statuelike.

He awaits the outcome of his efforts in suspended motion. As the ball rolls to the outside it starts to curve, ever so slowly. It picks up speed, and, approaching its mark, it quickly whips in and hits with a crash, sending pins flying in every direction.

The crowd's anticipation starts to build as our bowler explodes into animated actions, seemingly to exert some extra effort to make the last pin drop.

As 9 others lie in the wake of the ball, a stubborn 10-pin wiggles and shakes. Suddenly, it falls as our bowler drops down to one knee, his fists and teeth clenched. The crowd's resounding cheer echoes about the lanes.

He has met the challenge by getting his strike, to the delight of all who bowled it with him, every step of the way.

Yes, this is the excitement and joy of bowling! The precision and style of his every movement have been refined through hours of practice. He has taken his skills that one step beyond to achieve the distinction of being a "competitive bowler."

This book will provide the knowledge needed to make this transition and take that extra step in refining your game.

We are fortunate to have as our instructor the most competitive bowler in bowling today and of all time, Marshall Holman.

The winner of an exceptional 19 PBA titles in his young career, Marshall has brought to bowling the color and excitement the sport needed. His vitality to serve bowling's interests whenever called upon has made him bowling's ambassador.

He ranks number three on the all-time leading money winners list and held the highest average in the 1982 and 1984 PBA Tour while finishing second in total money won in both 1983 and 1984. In 1984, he was named *Bowling Digest*'s Annual Bowler of the Year.

Acclaimed by many as the best bowler in the world, and by others as the heir apparent to bowling's all-time crown, Marshall Holman gives, in this book, insight into what makes him a competitive bowler.

Whether you're a league bowler or pursuing the dream of a professional career, the skills outlined in the following chapters will improve your game and help you to enjoy more and compete more effectively.

1
ABOUT
MARSHALL HOLMAN

Our heroes perform their magic before our eyes, and we really think we know them. Unfortunately, however, we never get to understand and appreciate who and what they are.

To establish this relationship benefits both the fan and the performer, so that our momentary departures from reality have some meaning when we reflect on the endeavors in our own lives. We appreciate the successes we've gained so that our dream of aspiring to the lofty heights of our heroes' achievements serves as a source of *encouragement*, not *discouragement*!

As probably happened to many a youngster, my interest in bowling started when, at the age of 12, I watched the game on television. That telecast left me with a feeling that bowling was a fun activity.

I asked my father to take me down to the lanes so I could try it, and even today I can vividly remember the first game I ever bowled.

I bowled that first game at Medford Lanes in Medford, Oregon, on lane 25 with a score of 71, which by no means showed any promise of my ever achieving any type of prominence in the game. But after that first game I was hooked, so I continued to bowl, joining a junior league that took up all of my Saturdays. I really enjoyed it. I would bowl with the league, then I would continue to bowl afterward.

I was using house balls then because I didn't have my own equipment, and my hand used to get raw and bleed a little bit. When my right hand got too sore for me to continue, I'd bowl left-handed just to keep up the activity.

I enjoyed bowling. I found it was totally fun.

I was fortunate in those early days to be fairly good friends with the proprietor, Andy Anderson, who probably was as instrumental in helping my career as anyone because he gave me the opportunity to get down to the lanes.

I would do anything at the bowling center to be able to continue bowling: clean the ashtrays, sweep around, wash pins, or do whatever other odd jobs Andy had to offer. I was always hoping to be able to pick up some extra money (which really didn't pass hands) so I could do some more bowling.

Andy was probably getting the short end of the deal since the amount of work I did certainly didn't compensate for all the bowling I was doing!

This opportunity to be around the lanes on a continual basis gave me an intimate understanding of the sport. Not only was it great to do as much bowling as I did, but I also had the chance to watch the local star players and to grab some pointers from them—not by asking, but just by watching what they were doing and trying to incorporate that into what I was trying to do.

Having started to bowl at age 12 gave me a lot of catching up to do because most of the pros on tour today started bowling between the ages of 3 and 8 years, coming from bowling families. My family never bowled except for one year when my dad bowled in a league when they needed a fifth man at the radio station he worked for in Medford.

During those early years I enjoyed watching such stars as Harry Smith and Carmine Salvino because they were fun to watch, not only as great bowlers but also because they added entertainment to the game, along with their ability to throw strikes.

My parents weren't overly pleased with the importance I placed on bowling and the time I spent at the lanes, and their concerns were well-founded, considering the effect it had on my schoolwork.

Bowling was all I wanted to do. Fortunately, I was bright

enough (mind you, I'm not a genius by any means) to do a great deal of bowling while being rather neglectful of my schoolwork and still escape any real problems in school.

I do feel that parental support is important, though I didn't have it in those early years of my bowling. My parents, being rational people, didn't see any future in throwing a bowling ball, and, for the majority of people, there really isn't any. If I had children, and they were following the path I took to achieve status in the game of bowling, I would probably have to intervene and take them off the lanes a little bit because education is more important than bowling. This should be stressed to bowlers of all ages. I was fortunate to become a good enough bowler to come out on tour and make a fairly substantial living, but I still think that the chances that a youngster will make it all the way to the professional ranks are slim, and they're even slimmer that anyone will be able to make a living doing it. Many people have gotten a PBA card, come out on tour, tried it, and failed. There are few people who have come out and been successful.

I envy the guys who come out on tour at 24 or 25 and already have a bachelor's degree or another degree. This makes for a much more well-rounded individual, and I highly recommend that aspiring young bowlers follow this course. It's an insurance policy that you never have to renew, and it pays cash dividends!

After I completed school I worked around the lanes. I had some other jobs, but none of them really lasted long because I wasn't exactly the prime candidate for any of the jobs.

I remember one incident in which my parents got me an interview with a friend who was with the railroad. We were talking for a while, and things were really going along well when he said that the hours were such and such and that I would be required to work on some weekends. I stopped him right there and said, "Well, I can't do that. I have to have my weekends free to bowl." I'm sure that he was taken aback by that statement. He probably thought, "What's this kid trying to tell me? Here I am, offering him a job, and he's saying, 'No, I'm sorry, I can't work on weekends because I have to go bowling!' " Needless to say, I didn't get the job.

I'm sure he must look back now and laugh at our meeting, and he's probably glad that I didn't go to work for him.

Some fans probably feel I simply went out and bowled for a living, but bowling didn't come easily for me; I had to work extremely hard to make progress. I stopped bowling when I was about 13 because a friend of mine had taken me skiing, and I fell in love with that sport. So I missed the junior leagues when I was 13, spending my weekends on the slopes instead.

For some reason, bowling called me back, and I picked up where I left off. In the meantime, I had a wide variety of jobs. I worked for a steel company that made log forks for caterpillar tractors, and also made cabs for heavy equipment. Working in the paint shop, my duties were to remove the imperfections around the welds, which meant that I had to use a wire air brush and hard chisel. Unluckily, I had an accident with the air brush, cutting my left index finger severely. Fortunately, it didn't hurt my bowling hand.

As a maintenance person at a plywood mill, I cleaned the spreader machine, which glued to the wood a substance called Core that is in the middle of the plywood.

This was a disgusting job. The glue was very toxic and I would get glue poisoning. My arms would break out in rashes and it was tough. Fortuantely for me, the job didn't last very long and I went out on the tour very shortly after that.

None of these jobs lasted long because I was the type of kid who liked to joke around a little bit too much at the time.

I was so involved in bowling that I didn't really take any of them seriously. My job at the lanes was the only one I put any feeling into and cared about.

One thing I learned during that time is that employers have a strange inability to share any of your outside dreams, especially when they appear ever so remotely to affect your employment. They look at it as treason!

During my employment, I never articulated my feelings about bowling to others I worked with; even looking back now, I feel that if I had said something like that they would have given me my walking papers immediately.

JOINING THE TOUR

Despite my commitment to the sport, I never had any real aspirations to be a professional bowler. I just enjoyed bowling—it was fun. It wasn't until I was approached by a local businessman, when I was 19, that the thought really passed through my mind. He asked if I wanted to try the tour out.

It may sound strange to say that I had never really thought about it, but I was at a very indecisive stage in my life; I really didn't know what I wanted to do. I'd been out of high school for about 1½ years, and I didn't know whether I wanted to go to college or what I really wanted to do. But the opportunity suddenly arose to go out on the tour, and I figured, "Well, I can give it a shot for a year, and, if it doesn't work out, I'm only going to be 20 years old, and there are all sorts of things I can do."

That's when I first considered going out on tour. I think that another reason I hadn't considered going on the tour was that all I saw of the pro bowlers' tour was what I had watched on television, and I was very much intimidated by what I saw. I didn't feel that I'd have very much of a chance.

You have to consider the enormity of this step for me—to go out. It bordered on the monumental.

Living in a small town in Oregon is not like growing up in Los Angeles, Chicago, New York, or some other major city, where you can see professional sports firsthand. My image of a professional bowler was somebody who never made a mistake. I thought they were all godlike, which wasn't true at all. They're certainly very talented, but they make mistakes, just as I was doing at the time. They don't make as many mistakes as the average 180–190 league bowler, but they're still vulnerable.

Prior to going out on tour, I bowled in one tournament. There was a qualifier in my hometown, Medford, for one spot in the Portland Open in 1973. I won the qualifier and got a paid spot with some expense money to go up to Portland.

In the Portland Open, I was fortunate to make the top 24, but I spent most of my time in the top 24 watching the other guy bowl and wound up finishing—you guessed it—24th!

I was absolutely thrilled to have bowled in my first tournament and to have made the top 24 bowling against such stars as Don McCune, Dave Soutar, and other great bowlers of the time. It was certainly quite a thrill for me.

When I first went out on tour, knowing that it was my job, I was even more nervous than when I bowled in the tournament as an amateur.

I bowled very poorly my first tournament. I was paired on the same lane as Harry Smith, and he was one of the bowlers I had really admired as a kid because of his flair and great ability. I was so busy watching Harry and the other guys bowl that I wasn't concentrating on what I should have been doing. If I averaged 190 for that tournament, it was a lot.

It was an embarrassing performance, but, since nobody was paying attention to me, it was embarrassing only to me.

It served as a lesson, and I think it's something 99 percent of the people who come out on tour experience in their first tournament. So take a word of advice from a former experienced observer: Don't spend too much time concentrating on what everybody else is doing; spend more time on what *you* should be doing.

After a few weeks on tour I had to have a little talk with myself. I told myself, "The people I'm idolizing and spending my time watching started in the same place that I'm in. I have as much chance of becoming a good player on tour as anybody if I apply myself."

At the time, I didn't know how lucky I was to have a good solid game. If someone had asked me, "How good are you physically?" I couldn't have graded my game on a scale of 1-10. I did, however, get some good input from some of the players on tour. I know Don Johnson said that he was impressed with my physical ability. To have somebody like Don Johnson say, "Hey, kid, you look pretty good," certainly made me feel good and instilled more confidence in me.

THE CONTROVERSIAL IMAGE

Since I came out on tour, I've learned to bowl under different conditions in different centers around the country, learned how to cope with different kinds of lane conditions, and become a more consistent bowler from week to week.

During my first 13 tournaments on tour in the summer and fall of 1974, I cashed in on only four of them. In two of the four I cashed in on, I made the top five. At the time, this told me that maybe I had some good talent; maybe when things were going my way I could take advantage of that and get close to the top.

However, in nine tournaments I didn't make a dime, and you can't bowl like that. If you have that cash ratio, you can't make a living on tour.

My cash ratio now (in the last three to four years) is probably in the top three or maybe better. This has been a direct result of the biggest adjustment I've made: to be consistent from week to week.

However, I wasn't always consistent. Without a doubt, my

career has been controversial because of my style, and I'll be the first to admit it. Unfortunately for me, there was a time in my career that I could have cared less about what people felt or thought about me.

Back in the late '70s I was concerned only with what I was doing and really didn't care whether anyone liked me or not. But the Marshall Holman of today is much different because I *do* care. I've found out that it's much more enjoyable to have the people on my side, rooting for me, than to have them rooting against me. It's a blessing to have that positive energy that the fans can give, and they really help me out.

I wasn't trying to alienate the crowd in those days because I wasn't directing anything toward them. It was just my way of adopting an effective defense mechanism against my fellow pros, letting them know I wasn't afraid of anybody, that I was out there to do the best I could. This is how my image was created.

In those days, in the process of trying not to let the other pros know how inwardly uptight I was, I came off as very brash and cocky. Fortunately, after a couple of years on tour, cocky becomes confident. I must admit that I've matured, that I've become a little less volatile than I was in the past.

In order to be competitive, I have to be extremely intense! There are times when I'd like to be more easygoing about the way I approach my work, but I work a certain way, and that's the way I have to do it. There are some bowlers who could never work the way I do; it would disrupt them. But for me it's more calming to be excited and jumping around; it's something I have to do.

The more relaxed Marshall Holman is the real Marshall Holman I'd like to be on the lanes. I just haven't figured out a way to be as competitive as I want to be and be relaxed and just as easygoing when I'm working. Off the lanes, I'm really a rather calm individual. I don't go around beating my dog, and I lead a normal life off the lanes.

I don't really think I could change too much, although there are times when I wish I was a little less visible than I am today. For instance, that tournament in Milwaukee. I was pretty well hyped up playing against Mark Roth, starting with a couple of strikes. I got pretty excited, and then I got another double, and then the last bit of excitement I had was when I struck in the sixth frame for a double. I came up in the seventh frame and left a ringing 10, and that was about the last emotion that I showed because then I just kept on getting rapped (a term we use when you're getting tapped or you're making a good shot and you don't strike).

That Milwaukee house had a large capacity for spectators and some of these fans were extremely vocal. Their verbal abuse was directed toward me because I'm the one who's usually performing the extracurricular activities after I throw the ball. So they gave it back to me. So, there are times when I'd just like to be able to go down there and not have my reputation precede me, especially since my reputation has been blown out of proportion in many ways. I've been compared to tennis's John McEnroe, which I find quite a laugh because I've never really done the things McEnroe has done toward the fans. I vent my frustrations at the pins. I'm not yelling or cursing at a referee or telling people in the stands what they should do.

I don't know McEnroe off the court, so I wouldn't presume to judge him. He seems to take his job seriously, and so do I—but not to the same extremes.

Bowling is a competitive and difficult way to make a living, but it's what I choose, and it's what I enjoy. I may not look like I'm enjoying it all the time, but when I come back home and have a chance to reflect on what I'm doing I feel pretty good about what's happened over the last 10 years.

All is not "up" on the tour for any bowler, but, fortunately, I have a very short memory. I have the kind of temperament that lets me get upset in a hurry (it doesn't take a lot to get me upset while I'm bowling), but it passes quickly. If I qualify for the number one position for a telecast and I lose that particular game, I am certainly going to be upset and disappointed about not winning. But I'm not going to go to the next tournament and dwell on the fact that I had a chance to win and didn't. Instead, I'll go into the next tournament and do the best I can.

The same thing is true when things go poorly during a tournament. I may leave the lanes in a very poor frame of mind, but I come back for the next round with that being history and try to go on from there.

But you can never say never. In 1980, I was on probation. If you have three conduct fines on the tour in a calendar year and you get one more, you're automatically put on probation. I had about two weeks to go on my probation, and Mark Roth and I were bowling in the doubles in Las Vegas. We were bowling the title match on television against Pete Couture and Tommy Hudson. I was anchorman, as was Pete for his team. Up first, I was faced with their team leading by one pin going into our half of the 10th frame, and I was on a strike. The next strike was very important to put the pressure back on the other team. I didn't make a very good shot and left the bucket. In my anger or disgust, I kicked my foot out. Unfortunately, my foot caught the foul light on the lane adjacent to me, dislodged the foul light, and caused quite a little commotion.

I felt like crawling into the ball return. The commissioner was now under heavy pressure to come down on me very strongly. He thought about it for a couple of weeks and finally reached a decision to fine me $2,500 and give me a 10-week suspension. It's hard to say how much that 10-week suspension cost me. But if I multiplied my average weekly earnings for the year by 10 and added the $2,500 fine, it cost me somewhere between $30,000 and $35,000!

It wasn't just the money. The suspension sent me home at a time when I didn't want to go home; I really wanted to bowl. It was very difficult to have the organization say, "You can't play." It changed me greatly. Since then (because of it) I haven't wanted to bowl as much. After that suspension I wasn't able to stay out on tour for a great number of weeks consecutively until, perhaps, last year.

I think that now I've pretty well broken out of it, but for a couple of years I think it had such an effect on me that I didn't know what was happening. For sure, it's over now, and I get along really well with our commissioner, Joe Antenora. In fact, I get along with all the people who run the tour as well as or better than I get along with the bowlers and the fans. I consider the commissioner and the tournament directors my friends.

I'll never feel good about Joe's decision to fine me that heavily, but it's certainly nothing that can be changed—I can't go back and do anything about it. So, because of my short memory, it never really affected me when I was on the lanes. It did, however, have an impact on the number of weeks I could stand being out before taking a break.

My relationship with the fans has changed dramatically since that time, and my chances to do more exhibition work allow me to get closer to the public. In fact, I've heard many positive comments during my exhibition work, at press luncheons, and at other functions where I do guest speaking. People have come up to me afterward and said, "I didn't like you before I met you; just watching you on television or at a tournament, I didn't really like you very much, but now that I've had a chance to meet you in person, away from your competitive work, you're a nice guy and a normal guy."

THE SUPPORT OF FAMILY

But my biggest fans are my parents. They're very proud of what I've done, and they're very supportive. Even though I've achieved a certain level of success on tour, there still are times when there's a lot of frustration in what I do. So, if I have a bad tournament, I usually get in touch with them once or twice a week. They always have good things to say. Especially when I'm having a tough time, they're right there, saying, "You'll get 'em next week," and that helps. It would be very tough not to have them be supportive. Instead of being negative, they are always very positive, and I know that, living in a small town, they're constantly being asked questions about me. I think it's a source of pride for them.

That's one of the best things that can happen to you—to make your parents proud!

CAREER HIGHLIGHTS

I've been asked often to relate my most memorable career highlights, and there are three.

Being the youngest player in the history of bowling to win the Firestone Tournament of Champions gave me a feeling of extreme joy and accomplishment, winning on my first attempt.

In 1977, at the World Open in Chicago, I was bowling Pete Couture in the semifinal match on television, and I opened in the 9th frame, losing the lead I had held. Pete threw strikes in the 9th, 10th, and 11th frames and shut me out. Even the commentator, Jack Buck, who was doing the telecast with Dave Davis doing color, said, "That's it, Mr. Couture has won the match." Dave Davis said, "Wait a minute; he still needs seven pins, so it's not totally over." This matter of getting seven pins seemed to be a rather easy task. Well, Pete got five. When he got the five, I immediately jumped out of my chair, realizing that I had been given a fantastic reprieve. But I needed three strikes to win the game by one pin. It seemed to the people watching that it was a chance (a three-bagger) but not a great one.

For some reason I felt inside as if I had already rolled or thrown them. As soon as he gave me that opening, I felt I'd already made them and I was going to win the game. I threw probably the three best shots of my life, won that game by one pin, and went on to bowl Mark Roth for the championship. I struck in the first nine frames and went on to score 277 against Mark, winning the tournament. That was the biggest highlight and the most enjoyable of my career.

The win in Austin in 1983 also stands out since I hadn't won for two years. After going that long without a win, a good deal of self-doubt starts creeping into your mind. So, winning that tournament meant getting back on the winning track and was a fantastic lift for I went on to win the next tournament in Venice, Florida.

I don't think anything will ever touch what happened in the World Open in Chicago, in '77, though. That was when I came from absolutely nowhere to win the tournament. I had it, I let it get away, and then Pete Couture hit that head pin solid and got five pins, which very seldom happens.

I judge what's going on in bowling by what I see on tour, in our pro-am events, and by the number of people who come in to watch our bowling on tour, and I'm happy to report that it seems to be doing fairly well. We have great support, and our television ratings are excellent, being the best in our time slot for many years because of the amazing number of people who bowl. Such top players today as Mark Roth, Tommy Baker, and Mike Aulby are favorites of these telecasts.

THE FUTURE

I'd like to continue touring for another five or six years and then cut down the number of tournaments I bowl, for it gets very taxing, both mentally and physically, to tour full time. I've been on the tour for 10 years.

I'd like to get involved in local business around southern Oregon, for there are a lot of different options there. My hope is to continue to do exhibition work and to get to know more people on a personal level since I enjoy the feedback from that kind of situation.

My work with the organization for the Special Olympics is also important to me. I've been working with them for about two years.

When I'm home I get in touch with the organization, or they with me, and we meet down at the lanes to work with the kids. We just try to have a good time and not make it too complicated—not because the kids are handicapped, but because they're bowlers, bowling for enjoyment. I don't grade them, and, no matter who you are, you should enjoy bowling unless you're a professional, for then it becomes a job, although it may still be enjoyable.

I believe that all bowlers should bowl for relaxation and fun and should not put themselves under a good deal of pressure unless they are bowling competitively in scratch tournaments or even in some handicap leagues, where some of the fun can get away from you.

I'm fortunate to have a very strong physical game, a game that keeps me consistent from week to week, for there are really no lane conditions that I have a lot of difficulty with. I think it's up to me, mentally, how far I can go in bowling. It just depends on how strong I can stay and how much stronger I can become mentally, because I think I'm already in a very strong physical phase in my bowling career.

The way I play my game, I do certain things that happen so fast that I don't have time to catch them before they happen. I usually feel bad about having done them afterward. When I watch other players who tend to get a little upset in reaction to what they're doing, I know it's just not worthwhile. Once you've done something, you have to live with it. People have seen you do it, your peers saw you do it, and the rational Marshall Holman knows that it doesn't really do any good! So we try not to get upset and overreact.

Remember, good shot making will win out over luck in the long run, so prepare yourself to do your very best as you embark on this quest for bowling excellence. I wish you luck and wisdom in making your decisions in the sport you have chosen. But no matter what those decisions are, let them be made honestly within yourself and be new steps in a direction that will help to provide you with possibly a new and exciting way to make a living, but most of all to benefit you by assisting in making you a well-rounded individual.

Let's bowl!

2
ADVANCED CONCEPTS
IN BALLS, BALL ROLL, AND RELEASE

Once your ball is released, all the mental and physical adjustments you've made become a reality. For the advanced bowler, this reality can come as a shock, for the variables that must be considered, evaluated, and quantified often indicate only one proper means of execution. It is up to you to put them all together and sort them out (like a computer) within the least amount of time and to incorporate the proper adjustments with precision.

Bowling has been revolutionized in recent years with the introduction of new types of balls that aid bowlers in combating their never-yielding adversary, the lanes.

If you are going to progress to the competitive level, you must appreciate and fully understand the mechanics set forth in this chapter. The introduction of some new types of balls offers you alternatives you never had before to strengthen your arsenal.

To appreciate these alternatives fully, you must look at bowling as having two separate environments—one that is continually changing on the lanes (made up of lane condition and pin environment) and the environment behind the foul line that is created by your actions.

Let's start by examining the various bowling balls you can use.

TYPES OF BALLS

Three types of bowling balls are being used today:

1. polyester or plastic balls
2. rubber balls
3. urethane balls

POLYESTER

Polyester balls are available in three different hardnesses. The soft balls fall into a hardness range of approximately 77–80, with the most common polyester ball measuring 75–80. This ball is the one that is used most often on the tour. On the high end of the scale, balls can go as high as 89 in hardness.

The polyester ball was used exclusively on the tour up until a few years ago. Now its use on tour is reserved for when the lanes are hooking a great deal. When this hooking situation is evident, we use a mid-range or hard polyester ball, which allows your ball to go down the lane farther before biting on the lane since friction is reduced by the polyester ball.

RUBBER

The rubber ball preceded the polyester ball and comes in a range of soft and hard surfaces. Rubber is not used very often on the tour, but it can serve as a fairly good all-around ball, especially for amateur players. As a matter of fact, the soft polyester and rubber balls are both good for amateur players because they suit most conditions and don't overreact. It is when you have advanced in your level of play that other balls will make a big difference.

URETHANE

The ball that has really taken the tour by storm is the urethane ball. There are currently four or five manufacturers of this type of ball. Obviously, someone had a very good idea. Since most lane surfaces are being coated with urethane, why not make a ball out of the same substance? It certainly worked, for it has revolutionized the game of bowling, especially in the professional ranks, since about 1981.

This represents a major change; at one time 90 percent of the balls used on the professional bowlers' tour were the softer plastic balls. Now we see these being used only about 10 percent of the time.

Even though a urethane ball costs significantly more than the rubber or polyester, its versatility far outweighs the cost differential. (This is discussed further later in this chapter, under "Ball Fitting and Maintenance.")

UNDERSTANDING BALL CONSISTENCY

Rubber, polyester, and urethane balls each feature different consistencies, which will affect how they roll.

The rubber ball is made from a natural substance usually extracted from the rubber tree or other tropical plants. This natural substance then goes through a process of vulcanization to add to its strength, give it resiliency, and remove odor.

Polyester plastic balls are made of reinforced synthetic resin that is lightweight and strong. These resins are found in lacquers, varnishes, inks, etc. Sound familiar? Well, the lanes were covered with a varnish or lacquer; hence the ball's popularity. The distinction here is the synthetic origin of polyester (and urethane) and the introduction of many substances used to form the desired product through the process of polymerization.

The urethane ball comes from the chemical compounds that are formed esters that are organic compounds derived from living organisms. Again, a difference: there is more flexibility in adjusting the ball to the conditions of the game.

The chemical consistency of the urethane balls resembles the nature of the lane surfaces more than does that of the rubber or polyester balls, which apparently makes the urethane ball more compatible with the lane surface than the others. This probably is due to the interaction of the surfaces, allowing more or less friction to act for or against you.

This element is discussed in porosity of the ball's shell. When a ball is porous, it permits the entry of liquid through pores or little holes on the ball's surface. These holes can actually be seen when you look at a ball closely. The porosity of a ball allows it to hook.

The urethane ball is a porous ball. Consequently, the reason the urethane ball is receiving such high grades on the tour is its ability to hook more readily, due to its porous shell.

Even though the urethane and polyester balls are plastics, their individual qualities and properties make a world of difference.

BALL SPECIFICATIONS

Various tour rules govern the balls you use, from the types of materials used to plug them to the number of holes drilled in them.

HOLES

The maximum number of holes you can drill into your ball is six, and you must always use all but one hole for gripping purposes. With six holes, for example, at least five holes must be used for gripping purposes; if five holes are drilled, you must use four for gripping, and so on. Usually, an extra hole (one not used for gripping) is used to balance the ball.

HARDNESS

Your ball must measure at least 72 on the hardness scale. The hardness of a ball can be checked by using an instrument called a *durometer*. A small hole is drilled into your ball to determine if the outer shell has been altered.

WEIGHTS

Weights applied to a ball for balance purposes can have either a negative or a positive effect. These fall into six basic categories:

1. fingerweight
2. thumb
3. positive side weight
4. negative side weight
5. bottom weight
6. top weight

How much extra weight you can add is governed by the weight of the ball. If your ball weighs 10 pounds or less, this weight allowance is .75 ounce; for balls over 10 pounds, there is a 3-ounce limit.

The weight of the ball and its balance weight are determined by the "do do" scale that can be found in your local pro shop.

INSERTS

Any inserts you may add to your ball (described further later in this chapter) must be permanently glued in, and the material must be consistent with the material used in making the ball. You cannot use foreign substances on the outer coating of the ball to get better traction.

FOLLOW THE RULES

Since the rules governing bowling balls are strictly adhered to and enforced, it's important to ensure that your ball meets these standards. Generally speaking, after a ball is manufactured, you cannot materially change its features, such as hardness, biting, etc.

HAND GRIPS

Three basic grips can be employed to hold your ball:

1. conventional grip
2. semifingertip grip
3. fingertip grip

CONVENTIONAL

I recommend the conventional grip for all young bowlers because it enables you to hold the ball with authority by inserting your fingers up to the second joint.

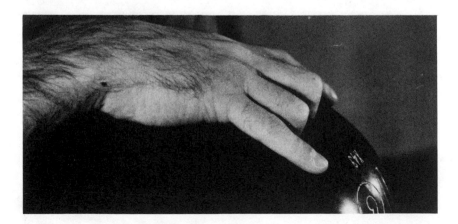

SEMIFINGERTIP

This grip increases the span or the distance between the thumb and the fingers. Here your fingers are inserted up to a point between the first and second joint. It is comparable to the grip used with a hand exerciser to obtain the maximum power and grip to squeeze it close together.

The advantage here is that the lift necessary in throwing a strong ball is enhanced and easier to employ with this grip. I highly recommend the semifingertip grip, as do most bowlers on tour.

FINGERTIP

Here the span increases further. Instead of inserting your fingers to a point between the first and second joints, you insert

them only up to the first joint of the fingers (the thumb is inserted all the way in all three grips).

You will have to get used to this grip. Your first reaction to it probably will be "How do I hold on to the ball?" After you become assured that it is possible, it can work for you.

Here the ability to achieve lift is increased to its optimum potential. If you're not getting the proper power from your ball, try employing other grips.

INSERTS AND THE HAND GRIP

Ball inserts basically serve two functions: (1) to protect your fingers and (2) to give you a better grip.

Different balls feel different to your fingers. By using inserts you can neutralize that difference and therefore use different balls without having to adjust your fingers to the change.

If you're having difficulty in holding the ball or maintaining proper comfort, you might try inserts to alleviate the problem.

Consistency is the byword when bowling on the tour, and having a consistently comfortable feel in the ball is just as important as using a consistent approach. The two work hand in hand.

BALL FITTING AND MAINTENANCE

Always have your ball checked by an experienced ball fitter. It's a science to fit a ball properly, and the results can be well worth the time and effort. Your hand can change in size after periods of bowling inactivity of varying duration, so when you start up a new season, go and have the ball checked to ensure a proper fit.

Among other things, a ball fitter will check the hole size, span, pitch, etc., in coordination with your style to give you the best possible fit on your hand.

This type of check can add pins to your game and comfort to your hand, reducing or eliminating the chance of injuries. Your investment will give you a feeling of comfort that all is well with your ball and eliminate any problems with it.

The ball's makeup dictates that you care for it, removing oil and other foreign substances to ensure that you are rolling the same-textured ball each time.

TIPS FOR THE URETHANE BALL

The urethane ball has a tendency to bite the lane a little harder than the plastic or rubber balls do. This is often just what you need as an advanced bowler faced with a perplexing lane condition, since this extra bite allows the ball time to react properly to the condition instead of overreacting.

Unlike the polyester or rubber balls, the urethane balls also can be sanded. If you take a light sandpaper, preferably a 400- or 600-grid paper, lightly sanding it makes the ball bite even more. The sanding does not damage the ball but allows you to increase its biting ability. After you sand the ball you can polish it, which will take the sand right off.

Urethane balls also seem to hold oil, so if they start to go straighter under heavily oiled conditions (reducing the hook), you can actually wash a urethane ball with soap and water to clean the oil out of it. By washing off the oil that has been picked up from the lanes you will restore the bite to your ball and regain the hook.

By following these maintenance tips, you can make a urethane ball act like three or four different balls. The cost is about 40 percent more than for rubber or polyester, but with the many uses and alternatives we've discussed the urethane ball becomes a pretty good buy.

BALL ROLL COMPARISONS

Assuming the same conditions—let's say the lanes have a fairly good concentration of oil on them—the hard plastic polyester ball is never going to pick up a roll and give you the power you will need. The results will be a ball deflection on contact with the pins instead of the ball's driving through.

The softer rubber ball would probably work reasonably well, but this ball has a tendency to hook a little early at times.

Let's review what *hooking early* means. The first 10–25 feet is the most critical portion of the lane in controlling the actual roll of the ball. This is an extremely important part of the game that for one reason or another is overlooked by some bowlers. This first 15–20 feet of lane is called the *heads*. If you can't control the heads, then you have no chance of controlling anything. You want the ball to slide through the heads and pick up a roll on the last 20–40 feet and then hook into the pocket. If your ball starts to roll early and hook early, your total effectiveness is diminished.

The screened area of the photo represents the heads.

The biting quality of the urethane ball proves its usefulness here by giving that edge to the bowler.

If I could carry only one ball on the tour, it would be the urethane at this point in time. I never thought anything would replace the polyester ball, and the polyester was the ball that did all the damage in the '70s and early '80s. For 10 years, the polyester was *the* ball, and it just didn't seem as though anything would come up to rival it.

I don't see a new type of ball on the imminent horizon, but I'm sure somebody will come up with something. It never ceases to amaze me what they do with equipment! All the manufacturers have become sophisticated in the last few years, defining their approaches. There used to be basically one company making top-of-the-line equipment, but the top ball is available from almost all manufacturers. I can't think of a company that doesn't have a ball out on the market or isn't getting ready to put one on the market. They're doing great things with bowling balls.

PLUGGING

One thing we're no longer allowed to do on the tour is plug bowling balls.

In the past, if I didn't like the way the ball was rolling or if I found a ball that I wanted to try, I would be allowed to put a plugging solution into the holes. The solution would harden, allowing me to drill right back into the ball.

The PBA doesn't allow plugging anymore, and it hasn't for about seven years. The reason it was disallowed is that this technique provided an opportunity to cheat. Bowlers could plug a ball and put lead, mercury, or other foreign substances underneath the plug and get a different reaction from the ball.

So, instead of trying to police that kind of tampering through the use of metal detectors on tour, where the ball actually had to go under the detector before use, it was decided to disallow the plugging of balls. I must admit the detector scene was a giant hassle.

What the prohibition has done is to make it a little more difficult for the tour's younger players, because it was much easier and cheaper to plug a ball than to buy a new one.

Many established bowlers have the luxury of manufacturers seeing to it that equipment is at their disposal, but for the younger players equipment can become expensive. Urethane balls cost about $100 each, with other balls running approximately $50–$70. So young bowlers can find it very expensive to keep themselves in equipment.

It's very important that you have access to a good deal of equipment. If you have only one or two balls, while other players have a dozen, it's like going out to the golf course with only a five-iron and a putter to compete against a golfer with a full set. You need a full complement of bowling balls to combat different lane conditions. If cost becomes a factor in your equipment outfitting, it will be only a matter of time before you feel the effects of this.

COMFORT

No matter what ball you use, it must feel comfortable in your hands. This may sound basic, but as in all sports the basics are usually the factors that are given too little priority and consequently affect the desired results. The comfort you feel will influence your control of the ball. If you feel uncomfortable, no matter what level you're bowling at, see a qualified person to make sure you have no obvious problems in ball fit or your physical game.

The ball must be an extension of your body to be thrown effectively. Don't suffer needlessly. Find out what's wrong and correct it.

SPEED

There are times during a match when you need to be able to throw the ball at high speed. Generally, when you're bowling late at night, lanes start to break down since lanes are oiled only once a day for us on the tour, contrary to popular belief. A good many people think they oil the lanes in between squads.

The lanes are usually oiled at 4:00 A.M. or 5:00 A.M.—the middle of the night. So, when you start there's a lot more oil, and you can throw the ball slower. As the day progresses, you have to throw the ball quite a bit harder to keep it from hooking high on the nose.

Likewise, there are some conditions in which you just can't move to the left and expect to find oil. Sometimes you have to stay in the same spot, utilizing the proper equipment to meet the condition or throwing the ball with more speed.

It's very important to be able to change speeds because this vital element minimizes the kind of moves you have to make laterally. It is easier to alter your speed than your position on the lane.

Earl Anthony was very good at making adjustments of speed. These adjustments were subtle, but sufficient to meet the situation.

I have the capacity to throw the ball very hard, which is really important, especially on the right-hand side of the lane. This is because the right-handers generally have to throw the ball a little harder at night than the left-handers because there are more right-handed bowlers than lefties, giving the right side of the lanes more work. My side (the right) is more tracked in and will dry up faster than the left side. Therefore, it's important to have this kind of adjustment in your repertoire of shots.

HOW TO OBTAIN SPEED

I don't believe the way to throw a ball harder is to take a higher backswing.

Competitive bowlers need to develop a feel for just how hard to throw the ball or how much force to apply to bring the ball through. To me, it's just a matter of finesse, a feel telling me just how hard I have to roll the ball. I don't speed up my approach or slow it down to throw it slower. It's just a matter of how I feel at the bottom of the swing and how much force is used coming through the ball.

This is the proper ball position in the bottom of the swing.

Some bowlers recommend taking an extra step or steps. In my case, this is impossbile since I start at the edge of the approach. Sometimes my heels will be hanging slightly over the edge of the approach. But some bowlers do employ this technique, while others use the big backswing. The only thing I can say is that to me it's strictly a matter of feel. By taking more steps, higher back-swings, or using other methods you are changing your natural

My hand crosses in front of my body as the ball is released, indicating that my swing is forced.

approach and lengthening your movements, and I believe this can only signal a chance for more negative things to happen.

Find what suits you best without dramatically altering your style and remember that this can only be done by experimenting.

TYPES OF ROLLS

It is very important for bowlers who wish to become competitive to know the options available to them. Of all the options outlined hereafter, I would teach only the semiroller.

This is the only ball I would want anyone to throw under today's conditions. This may change 5 or 10 years down the road because the game of bowling keeps changing, like almost everything else. But today's pins and game dictate using the semiroller. You cannot argue with success, and the tour should serve as your primary indicator.

HOOK

Many people have a misconception concerning what makes the ball hook. Most people feel that the reason a ball hooks is the spin on the ball, but that really isn't the main reason. The hook is obtained from the lift. It takes only a little bit of side roll; most of the hook is developed by forward roll with just a little side roll.

This type of release imparts forward roll.

This type of release imparts side roll.

PATH OF THE BALL: (from left to right) release ball in the heads, it approaches its mark (second arrow), and proceeds to roll toward its target . . .

. . . ball begins to hook (left) and goes into pocket.

When you see guys on the tour like Bob Handy, who really hooks the ball a lot (or, at times, me), you should know that the hook is accomplished by cupping the wrist forward, holding that position, and imparting more forward roll to the ball. Your hand will

The wrist is cupped on the backswing.

automatically come around the ball when you use this position.

If you put your hand down at your side and place your thumb at the 3 o'clock position and relax, it automatically goes to 12 o'clock on release, because it's normal to do so.

So, when they roll the ball, most people automatically come around the side of the ball. What you want to concentrate on is getting that forward roll. Again, the side roll will come automatically for most bowlers. It's that forward roll that people have trouble with, and that's where the power comes from. So the big crankers do not really get their power from the side roll, but from the forward roll.

STRAIGHT BALL

Nobody really throws the ball dead straight on the tour, but there are some bowlers who throw the ball almost straight. Two of the most successful are Mike Durbin and Ernie Schlegel, but they also lift behind the ball.

You should never overturn the ball; you should come through the back of the ball. You should feel as if your hand is splitting the back of the ball when you come through it. The most successful players on the tour are the ones who stay behind the ball most.

If you throw the ball and come around it (with your thumb), letting your elbow get away from you, this is called "chicken-winging" the shot. If you throw your ball in this fashion, you might get a hook, but it won't hook with authority.

When you can stay behind the ball, however, you can get some pretty good power. This is true even for Mike Durbin and Ernie Schlegel, who throw the ball very straight. They just don't hook that much, but they're coming behind their balls. I can't think of anybody who overturns the ball who's really been very successful on the tour.

So, the hook is really not the most important thing; getting behind the ball is. Failure to understand this keeps many good, advanced bowlers from achieving a competitive game.

When I learned how to throw a hook ball I felt I was learning the

Chicken-winging: right arm is far from side of body.

proper way, but I wasn't. I thought that the hook was developed through straight spin, so what I'd try to do is get up and throw my ball and top it. If I threw it slow enough, it would hook from topping it, but only momentarily, satisfying my desire for a hook, albeit ineffectively. It wouldn't, however, hook with any authority. The ball would hit very flat, but as I got a little stronger I was able to stay behind it (not topping it), and everything evolved into a strong game by my simply staying behind the ball. It can be that simple if you try. I can't emphasize this point strongly enough, for the results I speak about were a dramatic turning point in my game and competitive ability.

FULL ROLLER

The full roller is a dinosaur. You just don't see it anymore on tour.

There were some excellent full roller bowlers on tour; probably the best ever was Billy Hardwick. Bill was Bowler of the Year in 1963 and 1969. Hardwick's ball hardly hooked at all, but he could still bowl from all angles and be effective.

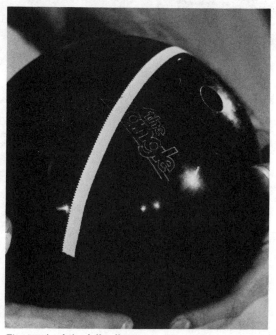

The track of the full roller.

The full roller is the ball that tracks in between the thumb and the fingers, the entire circumference of the ball. The lift employed in the full roller follows a path that is straight in an upward direction. It used to be successful for many bowlers, but it just doesn't work in today's game. With today's urethane lane conditions, the full roller doesn't have enough hitting power anymore.

FULL SPINNER

No one can bowl really well with a full spinner. You can throw a ball that tracks quite a distance below the thumb, but you can't full-spin it. I wouldn't recommend this ball roll for anyone. Its power is negligible since it involves employing only a wrist turn with no lift at all. The ball track is a feverish spin that alerts us further to its limited function, if it has any at all.

SEMIROLLER

This is the most frequently used and most productive way of rolling the ball. Here the ball tracks outside the thumb and the fingers and doesn't cover the full circumference of the ball.

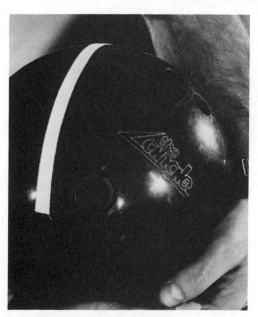

The track of the semiroller.

The semiroller is what everybody throws on the tour. The only difference among bowlers using it is that with some bowlers the ball tracks ⅛ inch from the thumb, and for others it tracks 1–2 inches from the thumb hole.

But to my knowledge everybody—both left- and right-handers— throws the semiroller today. The semiroller imparts a lift at an angle when compared to other ball rolls.

SEMISPINNER

This ball is not used much in professional bowling. There are a few bowlers who track a little lower than others, though.

Mark Roth used to throw a semispinner, about 10 years ago, and was fairly successful with it. But Mark really didn't start doing his best bowling until he switched to more of a semiroller.

Ted Hannahs, from Zanesville, Ohio, throws a ball that is closer to the semispinner than any of the other top pros today. Ted's ball still has good hitting power.

When you start tracking low, as in the semispinner, you lose a lot of the hitting power since you are essentially relying on wrist turn as opposed to lift.

Getting back to coming behind the ball to obtain good forward roll, as opposed to spinning the ball too much, it's just too easy to lose hitting power when the ball spins too much instead of rolling.

BACKUP REVERSE

I don't like to see this, but some people just naturally come around the ball in the reverse fashion.

A few good bowlers in the past have thrown backups or reverse hooks. One that comes to mind is a gentleman from Massachusetts, Eddie Hoestery, a right-hander. He was a very good bowler who threw the reverse hook. Another bowler, out of the Baltimore area, P. A. Anderson, also did quite well with it in the mid '70s. Both played lanes as if they were left-handed, with the ball entering the one-two pocket, as opposed to the one-three.

As far as being competitive from house to house, at a high level there's no way the backup reverse hook bowlers can keep up. It's just impossible.

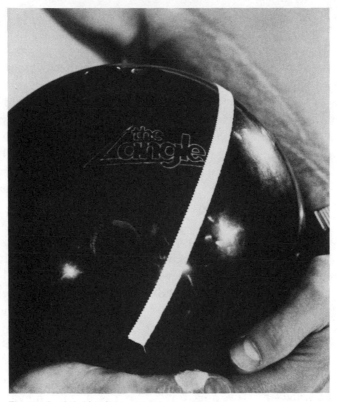

The track of the backup reverse.

Instead of imparting lift, the reverse backup ball sees the fingers moved to the inside of the ball. Again, power is questionable.

PIN CHANGES—BALL TRACKING

The pins we use are going to get heavier. The American Bowling Congress passed a new rule to have the pins weigh at least three pounds, six ounces. So, with the pins getting heavier, you're definitely going to need to have a higher-tracking ball. (The ball track covers that part of the ball's surface that touches the lane.) Applying this need for a higher-tracking ball to combat the heavier pins, the semispinner and the spinner would have too much deflection on the heavier pins.

Therefore, you must apply a consistent knowledge of ball tracking and ball roll to meet the challenge both on the lane surface and now at the other end of the lanes (with the heavier pins).

By now you must realize that the techniques that make an advanced bowler competitive are totally interrelated, with various factors such as lane conditions affecting ball roll, etc. This overlapping is essential since it supplies you with a bridge, very much like a computer, to accept and translate programs written in different languages. Our purpose is to gather all the variables, as we said before, to evaluate and assess the proper skills to execute.

RESULTS OF PIN CHANGE

As a result of using heavier pins, I see bowling averages going down across the board, from average bowlers up through the professional ranks. The reason averages will go down a little bit is that bowlers won't get the same side board action they got with the lighter pins flying up and to the side. The pins will be a couple of ounces heavier each, causing them to die in the gutter. They won't come out of the gutter; if they do so at all, they won't come out as strongly as they used to.

In the past 10 or 15 years the game has become rather easy in terms of knocking the pins down. So it's a bold move by the American Bowling Congress to adopt these new standards. The change is like taking candy away from a child. Bowlers have had it relatively easy in the last 10 years or so, with manufacturers coming up with pins that have double voids—lighter and much livelier.

With the heavier pins, the scores will just be going down. It's going to happen to everyone, so I don't think any one group has any right to complain over it; it's just going to be a fact of the game. The result of the new standards is that there will be more of a premium on good shots, which is good for the game.

We can only hope that this change will not have an effect on the popularity of the game, but I'm sure that a lot of league bowlers will be talking to their proprietors about it. When the averages start going down (not a lot, but a little) everybody will be affected at least a pin or two a game, and there's going to be a little bit of controversy when it goes into effect.

I guess some proprietors will establish a night of lighter pins to build some interest and set up a comparison. It may prove interesting.

BALL ROLL REVIEW

CUPPING THE WRIST

It's essential to have a strong ball roll, but not necessarily a large hook. Strong roll comes from a good lift through the wrist more so than from the fingers imparting the roll. When your wrist is in a cupped position you can impart more roll as you come from behind and through the ball.

It is imperative that you be versatile enough to change your hand positions to meet the situations presented on the lanes.

The less you cock your wrist toward your body, the less power you will be getting. So, if the lanes are hooking more, I might drop my wrist down an inch or so and try to come through the ball a little bit softer.

Lift is imparted to the ball at release.

The wrist is cupped on the backswing.

THE POCKET STRIKE

If you have developed a good ball roll, you have made the pocket larger. The larger you make the pocket, the greater the margin for error you allow yourself and the easier it is to throw strikes.

Conversely, many lower-average bowlers have what looks like a relatively good hit, but their ball deflects and fails to carry through to the 5 pin or leaves the 8-10.

So it's the guys who throw the stronger ball and hit in that pocket who just clear the pins off the lanes.

It's important to have some kind of a strong rolling ball—accuracy will only take you halfway.

HAND POSITIONS

To overcome the problems connected with the development of a strong ball roll to complement your accuracy, you can experiment with hand positions. By holding the ball a little stronger or using one of the many different wrist devices, you can find a way to increase your effectiveness.

There are many wrist devices that are used to put pressure on the back of the hand and keep the wrist in a stronger position. Many of the pros use these devices. I don't use the wrist devices very often because my ball is naturally strong.

These devices provide an ideal way to learn how to throw a strong ball, and you will get a little more roll with it. A wrist device is intended to help you achieve a strong wrist position. It's like having the habit of fading the ball in golf. If you take your right hand and turn it over clockwise, that will make you turn over the club face a little, but at release, instead of fading it, you might start hooking it. That's what these wrist devices are designed to do.

You might come to depend on them, but that's not bad if you're getting results. Many bowlers on tour use certain wrist devices exclusively and constantly, and there's nothing wrong with that at all.

Some people need the little reminder that a wrist device provides. A little reminder is basically what the devices offer since they're not all that rigid on the whole. A couple are very strong, but for the most part they're just reminders.

In my case, wrist devices would hamper my adjustment to some lane conditions. I find most of them restrictive, but for the amateurs (and this is the market that they were primarily designed for) it's a good piece of equipment. By using this device, an amateur can impart the same roll as a professional gives to the ball. I think it's well worth the cost to try them out.

BALL PATTERNS

You want the ball to skid or slide through the heads, then to pick up a roll and hook into the back end. If your ball is hooking too early, you lose all control by not controlling the heads.

I bowled with an amateur in the pro-am once, and his ball was hooking immediately upon hitting the lane. It would start hooking and then roll out. So he had absolutely zero power.

Again, the ball should slide, then start to roll and hook. If it starts to hook too soon, the chances of hitting the pocket with any power are almost nil. It's the same whether you throw a big hook or whether you throw the ball fairly straight.

I think most bowlers don't understand this, and it holds them back from establishing a competitive game. In their efforts to hook the ball, all they're doing is hooking it early. Hooking the ball early takes all the power and accuracy out of the game. You must delay the roll by doing a number of things.

DELAYING THE ROLL

Throw the ball out on the lane a little bit, lofting it farther to delay the roll as shown in the photos below.

You can try using a harder ball, made of rubber, polyester, or even harder urethane. I don't really suggest the hard urethane because that's a ball that should be used by the pros, and even the pros should not use it all that often to correct this kind of problem.

The hardness of the ball can aid you in getting past the heads without experiencing problems. Remember, to deliver the ball properly, slide, roll, and hook.

THE FALL-BACK SHOT (FOURTH ARROW)

This is a good shot that you shouldn't play often because lane conditions don't always warrant it.

The fall-back shot from the fourth arrow involves actually starting the ball on the nose; it's not really heading into the pocket. It's actually lying in the pocket or even coming back and finishing

FALL-BACK SHOT: the release and path of the ball to pocket.

to the right a little bit. It seems as though it wouldn't hit very hard, but under some lane conditions you can throw the ball almost right at the head pin, and the ball will actually back off a little at the back end. When the shot is there, it's a very comfortable shot for me to play, but I don't see it very often.

If you try a fall-back shot with success, you'll find you can line up to hit flush or you can line up a high flush all day.

Since you are executing this shot from the fourth arrow, you are now in a position deep inside. The ball follows a left-to-right path as it straightens out toward the pocket.

THE SWING SHOT (THIRD ARROW)

This is my favorite shot! You're still inside (as in the fall-back shot), where I like to play, around the third arrow or even deeper.

THE SWING SHOT: the release, approach to the mark (third arrow), and path of the ball to the pocket.

Here you start the shot at the third arrow, swing the ball out to around the second arrow, and then hook it back in with a lot of power to get a good deal of pin action.

THE LINE BALL (SECOND ARROW)

I'm not very good at this shot at all. This shot's more in the line of Nelson Burton, Jr., and Mike Durbin, who are very good at keeping the ball right on line, just letting it break a little bit at the back end. The pattern here is to roll the ball over the second arrow in a straight line toward the right of the pocket just a bit. It should break toward the pocket at the back end. Since most bowlers are not able to accommodate this line, they experience difficulty with this ball.

I don't look for this shot too often. It's very difficult for someone who hooks the ball a lot.

THE POINT SHOT (FIRST ARROW)

The point shot is very much like the line shot from the second arrow. It can be played from almost anywhere. You can start the ball from the gutter or from the one to about the twelfth or thirteenth board, pointing it up toward the pocket. This is a shot played by people who throw the ball straight, like Durbin or Ernie Schlegel.

Durbin or Schlegel probably would play this shot up the boards from, say, the first arrow or 8 or wherever it might be. I would probably be using the second arrow or maybe even deeper, around 12. So what you try to do is get the breaking point down the lane.

Now, if the breaking point isn't coming until 40 or 45 feet, but they're starting up at the pocket, I'll throw the ball out and try to hook it back.

So, it's almost like during one point the ball is at the same spot 45 feet down the lane. We're looking for the same spot at 60 feet, that pocket on the 17th board.

So here I've adjusted my skill to a particular situation, where I have to use the hook to get to the pocket and they have to throw the ball straight. Again, this is not totally straight, but with just a couple of boards' hook, where I may be using seven or eight boards to hook.

COORDINATING BALL ROLL, RELEASE, AND PATTERNS

You must be able to adjust your game to where your natural hook patterns will come in at the best angle. Here again, we're overlapping into the topic of lane conditions.

The most important key is what your ball is doing in the first 15 or 20 feet, because if you have control over the heads then that will give you more area to work toward the pocket.

BACK ENDS

Very seldom will you find bowlers worrying about the back ends. The only time you worry about the back ends is when the heads are in bad shape and the ball is hooking early in the heads. If the oil carries down and you're not hooking in the back ends, you have a real problem.

But, if the back ends are tight and the heads are fairly tight (that is, there is oil and the ball is not hooking a lot), the heads aren't hooking much and the back end is hooking you can be all right with that.

If the heads start hooking, then you're in trouble. This problem happens quite frequently on the tour. Fortunately, there's a way to combat the situation. You can throw the ball almost over the heads. Loft the ball out an extra two to four feet if they're really hooking a lot. You can also go to the harder ball or throw with more speed.

One of the greatest bowlers in controlling the heads was Barry Asher. Barry left the tour in the '70s when, as far as I was concerned, he was in his physical prime as a professional bowler. He was one of the all-time greatest bowlers ever, but he just didn't enjoy it or want to do it anymore. It sure made it easier for the rest of us.

The concepts of ball roll and release are an integral part of your game. You must be able to understand exactly what your ball is doing as it goes down the lane so you can make the proper adjustments. A small error on the line, like missing your spot, can cause disaster 60 feet down the line. If you don't know why it happens and how to correct it, you'd better go back and practice. The effort you put out will improve your games.

3
ADVANCED TECHNIQUES
FOR APPROACHING STRIKES, SPARES, SPLITS, AND TAPS

Don't let anyone fool you; bowling is a strategy-oriented game that requires its competitors to know exactly what position they are in at any given time during the game and to assess what it will take for them to win.

Like a computer, the bowler must digest an inordinate number of variables that control bowling's environment, assigning values to each for his next shot. Then, with the ease of a well-oiled machine, he must patiently execute his choice, and, along with the fans and his opponents, await the result of his analysis.

As the drama unfolds, he explodes into jubilation, as his choice is proven right.

With this in mind, you must appreciate the important relationship that each ball has with the next, and you must use the available adjustments that can be employed to obtain the desired result.

Let's expand our bowling knowledge of strikes, spares, splits, and taps beyond the fundamental stage to add a new dimension in our computer bowling bank—the mind!

THE CHALLENGE OF EACH SHOT

Every time you pick up your ball and approach the lane, you're embarking on a new adventure. If you think that each roll is like the next, then you're obviously not concerned with becoming a competitive bowler.

The advanced bowler wishing to achieve the competitive game enjoys the challenge as each ball is thrown. Every new condition must be met with intelligence and skill.

Every shot is a work of art, for nothing can be taken for granted; a single pin left standing is not a spare until you knock it down.

All too often, bowlers lose their composure when they haven't bowled a strike and come up for their next ball in a poor frame of mind, just winging the ball out so that it misses its mark. This costs them not only an open frame, but probably the match in many instances, since regaining this composure is essential and is not an easy task.

This is but one simple example of the wrong approach to a situation and the consequence that follows.

The mindset you need when approaching the lane is to strike every time. Realistically, however, you and I know this is not going to happen. When it doesn't happen, you must let history be history and move on to the next ball, where your best shot is a spare. By approaching your bowling game in this fashion, you have found probably the only formula that will enable you to develop advanced techinques in approaching strikes, spares, splits, and taps. A concept as simple as bowling one ball at a time, each being your very best, will help you achieve the results you want, especially if you're thinking throughout.

The reward you get from such an approach is satisfaction—and, in the pro ranks, professional satisfaction—that you've done your very best.

The goal—to knock down all the pins—might seem pretty basic, but the way in which you must achieve this desired result may not be so easy. Nothing is really simple in a sport where the environment on the lanes and behind the foul line is constantly changing as a game goes on.

Your ability to meet each of these situations, whether you need a strike, a split, a spare, etc., is the element that separates the mediocre player from the one who will develop into an accomplished bowler.

KNOW YOUR BALL

To achieve the ability to bowl more effectively, you must know the ball you throw and the amount of hook you can expect each time within the slightest deviation. If your ball is not following an acceptable and predictable pattern, you're obviously losing control, and you'd better find out why in a hurry, for to proceed any further may prove to be an extremely frustrating endeavor.

Every bowler must know what to expect. You've reached this stage in the sport not by luck, but with an effort that combined skill and knowledge. Therefore, refining your game demands a greater sensitivity in order to develop the other element you seek. That element—*implementation* of your skill and knowledge— works in conjunction with the other two, forming a total relationship and commitment to the sport.

Implementation is simply the act of doing exactly what your skill and knowledge are intended to enable you to do. Implementation requires you to be mentally and physically ready to bowl that best shot every time, by using all the skills you have.

If you don't implement or put into action those skills, the results of your actions will be less positive than you desire. This is true as you step up to the line to bowl your strikes, spares, splits, and taps.

Implementation is a transparent quality that none can see or even determine from talking to you. You can see skill executed and hear knowledge expressed, but implementation can only be likened to an atmosphere that you create, which allows you to do your very best every time you deliver the ball. It's seen in the results you get and in your rising scores. It's the element that makes the difference between getting the job done and just thinking or talking about it.

PIN VS. SPOT BOWLING

As you know, there are two ways to acquire a high level of bowling accuracy—pin bowling and spot bowling. Advanced bowlers would definitely want to go with spot bowling, whether they're spotting at the dots or the arrows or even further down the lane. I would be surprised if anyone reading this book is a pin bowler. The majority of advanced bowlers are spot bowlers, and the amount of success attributed to this technique far outweighs that of pin bowling.

Sighting the pins.

If any of you out there are pin bowlers, I urge you to go with spot bowling because it's much easier to be accurate with a spot that's 10–20 feet down the lane than to try fitting the ball into the pocket 60 feet down, sighting at the pins.

The same theory applies to shooting a rifle. No one would think of attempting to aim at a bull's-eye without a sight on the rifle. To aim 50 or 100 yards away with the naked eye is asking too much of even the person with the best visual acuity.

The spot or arrow acts like the sight on the rifle, allowing you to line up your shot and guide its path.

KEEP YOUR EYES ON THE BALL

It's important that your eyes never leave the mark until the ball has passed over it. If you're concentrating on the mark and pick your head up too soon, there is no way you're going to be accurate each and every time. Accuracy is not a coincidence, but the result of your effort to sight your mark, concentrate on it, and control your ball's path to the target.

Some bowlers, and rightfully so, will watch their ball a bit beyond the mark before lifting their eyes. This practice can prove quite enlightening in identifying what your ball is doing in those first critical moments of contact with the lane.

The ball passes over the second arrow—always follow the line of your ball with your eyes.

It is here that the first assessments of lane conditions, discussed in Chapter 5, start. So be alert and spend the time to look at your mark and beyond.

Speaking of beyond, some bowlers actually aim farther down the lane at a spot they pick out. It may be a darker board or another easily identified element that they can concentrate on. Here your line of sight is longer and your gaze is held longer until the ball passes over it.

An advantage of this method is that it forces the ball to hook a little later. When you pick a spot farther down the lane, your follow-through will be sustained a little longer, thus keeping the ball from hooking early.

If you find that your hook is high and to the left while bowling the spot 15–20 feet down the lane, you might try to develop a spot that sits farther away so that you eliminate the early hook.

BOWLER'S TRIANGLE

When sighting your spot, it might be helpful to think of your sight in terms of a triangle whose base rises vertically from the lane (the bowler's triangle). Your spot is the end of the triangle,

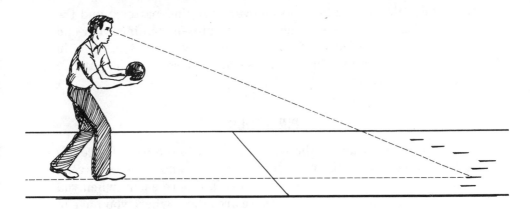

with the two other points being formed by your line of sight and a straight line drawn from the outside of your right foot.

As you approach the target, the triangle becomes smaller, and as you crouch to release your ball, maintaining eye contact with your spot, your ball will be traveling through on your right side, following a comparatively straight line. If you drift from the path of your foot's line to the mark, your eye contact with the mark should keep you on target. Any adjustment at the foul line can be stabilized by extending your right hand straight out to the side on release. Your hand will follow through to the mark as your eye continues contact. As your ball passes over the mark, the triangle is completed.

The remainder of your shot is up to your ability to control your ball.

Remember, the pins are 60 feet in front of you and are also arranged in a triangle, so the establishment of your bowler's triangle at the other end certainly makes sense.

THE THREE ENVIRONMENTS

The importance of the three environments that exist on the lanes cannot be overemphasized. They are the physical environment behind the foul line, relative to your physical game; the lane

conditions that are subject to an ever-changing pattern; and the pin environment, where the action of the pins determines your end result. These 10 objects of your efforts, as we will see, come in varying qualities and have a personality of their own that you must be acutely aware of.

PIN ACTION

You must be aware of the way pins react to the ball. There are different weights to the pins; some are dead, and some are lively. You've got to know whether some pins fall more easily when you come light in the pocket and if there are others where you have to hit deep in the pocket in order to strike. It's important to be aware of that and not just concentrate on what the lanes are doing. Watch the way the pin action is working to know whether you can give it a free swing and let the pins rattle around at will or whether you're going to have to be a little bit clearer with your shot and fit it deeper into the pocket in order to carry the solid strike.

DRIVE OF THE BALL: The ball hits the pocket, drives through the pins, and clears the deck as a result of its drive.

BALL DEFLECTION: Ball hits head pin and deflects to right, striking the 3 pin. Note how the head pin goes right instead of driving through the rest of the pins.

You must watch your ball entering the pocket and watch the way it either drives through the pocket or is deflected by the pins.

If the pins are the master over the ball, then you're going to have to go for a deeper shot into the pocket.

It's fairly easy to tell the different kinds of pin action that pins of different weight and different manufacturers take, since all have different characteristics that make them react differently.

Watch the ball enter the pocket. If you're pretty sure you've made a good shot and your ball deflects, leaving a weak 10 pin (or a weak 7 for the left-hander), the chances are that you're not going to be able to carry that type of hit. You'll have to make some small adjustments, moving yourself a little bit to the right, giving the ball a chance to hook into the pocket a little deeper.

On the whole, heavier pins will not give you a lot of action. Their weight reduces this, as seen in the new pins we discussed that will be introduced by the ABC. On the opposite end, the lighter pins will mix more, creating a higher-scoring condition. Your identification of the amount of mixture and life is important, as we said, to determine the kind of hit required.

The way the pins go down and which are left standing are also really important factors. They're like signs to guide you to what's ahead for your next shot.

Here, we are getting into a highly technical area that, like lane conditions, requires you to be mentally alert and physically ready to adjust to anything that happens. Except here, your ability to read visually what's going on 60 feet away is critical to determining the proper adjustment.

Let's take it step by step. Your ideal hit is the pocket of the 1-3, so common sense dictates that anything less will result in a different reaction by the pins.

STRIKES

Quite simply, the object is to knock all the pins down. When you do so, you've accomplished 100 percent of the skill-knowledge-implementation relationship we discussed earlier. When any one of these three elements is not at peak perfection, your perfection down the lane is affected accordingly.

The ideal hit in the 1-3 pocket is not the only hit that produces strikes. The 1-2 pocket on the left side can produce the same result, along with the thin or mixer strikes that delight the fans. Naturally, other uncertain hits result in strikes much to our bewilderment, but no one questions the good fortune of the game.

It is therefore important that every potential strike ball you throw result in a pocket hit with the proper speed and power to assure maximum results. Don't count on luck to make up for sloppy bowling. Sooner or later, it will run out—usually at the most inopportune time.

PIN ACTION

What actually happens when your ball hits the 1-3 pocket? First of all, your ball hits at precisely the midpoint of the bottom of the pin.

The spot on the pin where the ball hits is important since this determines the way in which the pin will react.

When the ideal hit occurs in the 1-3 pocket, the pins are hit slightly to the right of center, which is the *nose* of the pin. The

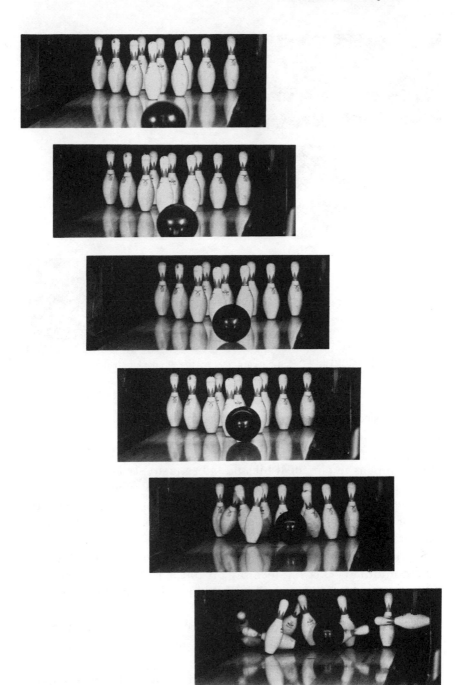

IDEAL HIT STUDY: ball starts to hook, hooks further toward the pocket, whips into pocket area, right on target, drives through, and causes maximum pin action . . .

IDEAL HIT STUDY CONTINUED: full pin mix occurs, the pin deck is being cleared, and the result is the ideal pocket hit.

pocket is broken down further into three specific subareas, evidencing a high, middle, and light hit.

Ideally, a proper hit is a middle-pocket hit on the 1-3, so let's see what happens in our ideal hit and subsequent strike.

The 1 and 3 pins will be taken out by the ball, while the 3 takes out the 6, 9, and 10, and the 1 takes out the 5, driving to the 9-10 as your ball drives through. The resulting pin action takes care of the remaining pins.

So a lot depends on the action of the pins. If you hit the 1-3 in less than a middle-pocket hit, let's say off to the right of the head pin, you are going to be hitting the 3 fully, resulting in the likelihood that it will miss the 10.

The cause of this deviation can be many things that result in the ball's entering the pocket at a different angle than is desired to hit the 1-3 in the middle of the pocket.

When you see this type of action taking place, you must adjust your hook and angle to attain the proper point of entry. If you are unable to make this adjustment, you will continually leave pins, and this can only lead to lower scores and frustration.

The way the ball enters the pocket is a significant guide to the way the pins react, for a good hit will tell you the mix of the pins while a lighter hit will tell you a lot about the pins' weight and ability to assist you in making the strike without a clean 1-3 middle-pocket hit. These, as discussed before, are the results of thin, mixer, or crossover strikes.

Another consideration in striking is the area at the pocket, which means that, if you hit high, medium, or light in the pocket, your ball will carry and you'll get the strike.

Correspondingly, if someone says the area on the lane, it refers to being able to miss your mark (arrow or spot) on the lane by a board or two and still come up for the pocket hit.

Obviously, both of these conditions depend on the conditions of the lanes that create them.

BALL ACTION

Don't think that every 1-3 hit will produce a strike. This is just not so. The lane's condition may have an effect, but if this is not the case, then you have to look to your ball action. If your ball is not driving through, going from right to left to pick up those pins we discussed in our ideal strike, it's not going to strike. It's essential to understand that the ball has a direct function in knocking down the pins.

You must check various physical characteristics when you're not striking or getting the action you want.

Run through this small checklist to evaluate what's going on.

1. Check your wrist. Is it:
   - firm?
   - behind the ball?
2. Are your fingers lifting?
3. Are you topping the ball?
4. Is your follow-through complete?
5. Check your speed.
6. Check your arm swing.

Your answers to the checklist questions should result in some solutions to your problems.

Now, make the adjustment and watch the pin action. If you're successful, great. Your search is over. If not, try again, using this experience to eliminate some of your problems.

Just as you go through a mental checklist for lane conditions and the physical game, you must also apply this theory to the type of action you're getting on the back end. This can be done only if you pay close attention to those pins and the way you make the hit and their reaction to the hit.

EQUIPMENT

Keep an open mind with regard to where you're going to play on the lane and the type of equipment you're going to use. It sometimes takes a gamble to achieve the desired result.

You can do quite a bit with the new urethane balls to aid your game.

If your ball is hooking too much, you can simply walk over to one of those polishing machines that almost every bowling center has, and polishing your ball will make it go a little straighter down the lanes. That is probably the simplest adjustment you ever will make. If you know that you're moving into an alley that hooks a lot, you might make sure you use that kind of machine to prepare your ball.

Early in 1984, Larry Lichstein, our players' service representative, who handles our locker room on the pro tour (and also a traveling pro shop), purchased one of those machines, and it's at the bowlers' disposal to adjust their balls at the first sign of an over-hooking situation.

Years ago, when I first started bowling, I thought of the Brunswick machine, "The Lustre King," as just a way to make my ball look good and not as a way to give me a little different option as I bowled.

Likewise, the wiping of the ball I've mentioned plays a significant role in reducing the incidence of problems because of substances the ball picks up as it rolls down the lane.

I wipe my ball with a towel each time to remove the lane oil so I can get a consistent read of the lanes as I'm bowling. There are some bowlers who don't wipe the oil off at all, and I can't understand why not.

The reason for my exercise is actually twofold: (1) to get a

At left, I apply rosin to holes of my ball, then I wipe it clean of oil from the lane while spinning with my left hand.

consistent roll on the ball and (2) to keep the lane conditioner off my hands, because it can be very difficult to make shots if you have lane conditioner on your hands.

These and other small precautionary measures pay many dividends to the bowlers who observe them. The conscious bowler, who is aware of their existence and implements them, will have the edge.

Those less-than-desirable pocket shots, whether they be light, high, or whatever, give us an opportunity to discuss our next topic—their by-product, the spares.

SPARES

Again, let's focus on the pin itself. As we saw, the pocket was located slightly to the right of the nose of the pin at center. Since the actual pocket of the pin is only about three inches in length, any deviation from the direct center of the pocket will create a much different result in pin action.

You must understand that, even when you hit the pocket, hitting it in different places creates different pin action. The pocket has a high-middle-light range, so the type of hit will determine the result.

The hit creates *deflection*. The amount of deflection a pin makes causes it either to miss pins by going around them or, in the case of a good hit, to drive through the pack powerfully, taking more pins with it.

Unfortunately, the result of your effort is not always a strike. Your pins may deflect around others, or your ball may not drive through the pins but will deflect itself.

What you must do is determine which situation exists. If the pins are deflecting, your hits have to be more direct in the pocket. If the ball is failing to drive through the pins, then you need power. In each case, you've determined why you are not getting the desired result and identified the adjustment necessary. The next step is translating this decision into action.

Some hits are to be avoided, since their pin action can create some very hard or impossible spares to make. One such hit is the nose hit.

NOSE HIT STUDY: ball approaches the pins, cuts across to the head pin, hits it but misses the 1-3 pocket, carries to the left, restricting pin action. Further pin action

removes the 10 pin, but the 6 pin is left.

The nose hit moves you out of the 1-3 pocket, hitting solidly on the nose of the head pin. The resulting leave combinations are an indication of the trouble this type of hit brings. The combinations are the 6-7, 3-6-10, 6-7-10, 4-6-7, 4-6-7-10, and more. We will discuss other leaves of this type of hit in detail later.

We now understand that spares are the result of the pins' deflection away from and out of the path that would determine a strike.

Let's return to those zones on the pin to get a better idea of the pin deflection and spares.

If you hit the head pin on the light area of the pocket, a 7-pin spare could result. Hitting the head pin high could leave a 4-pin spare. So the area of the head pin that you hit clearly indicates what you leave and correspondingly what you're doing wrong.

Your adjustments can be quite refined, if you're an accomplished pro. For example, on a 7-pin spare, you can adjust your line to come into the middle pocket and avoid the light hit. Your ball may be breaking a little late, so your adjustment can be refined to that degree.

Moving farther to the right of the head pin, that area is called the *bucket.* A hit in the bucket area will result in a bucket leave— the 2-4-5-8 or various other leaves such as the 2-4-5, 2-5, 2-8, and 2-7.

No matter what area you hit on the head pin, the results will tell the tale. It's up to you to be able to read them.

BUCKET HIT STUDY: ball hits the 1 pin lightly on the right side and is deflected away from the rack.

CONVERTING SPARES

I think it's important that you realize that you don't have to overpower most spares. Sparing is more a game of accuracy than a power game. For example, if you leave a single-pin spare, it's totally an accuracy situation.

Strategy

You might want to go with a little more speed and a little less hook, no matter what spare you're shooting at.

A great many bowlers on the tour use this kind of strategy when shooting spares. Probably the best spare shooter in the game today is Joey Berardi. If you were to watch him, you would note that he throws the ball fast and straight at virtually all of his spares, except for where there is a sleeper or double wood (a pin right behind another pin), where you need some kind of power to get out the back pin.

But then again, some people instruct you to throw the very same ball in bowling spares as you do in bowling strikes, on the theory that this method will ensure that your delivery doesn't become confused with the two different ball rolls.

Since this represents two schools of thought, you must make the decision based on the results you get and on your particular style and ability.

The use of the hook can cause you to miss some spares, and I feel that every spare missed results in 10 pins lost in your game. I don't know any bowler who is willing to sacrifice that number of pins. So make your decision wisely.

I can only say that I recommend that you cut the hook if you throw a large one, to allow a greater degree of accuracy to come into play.

Relying on power to make a spare is where a lot of very talented young bowlers get into trouble.

Remember, no matter what the spare is, don't take its conversion for granted. All too often an easy spare will turn into a red face as an overly relaxed bowler approaches this task with an indifferent "it'll be easy" attitude. They're all hard until you make them. Don't throw away a spare because of carelessness. You've missed the strike; now make the spare. It's your last chance in the frame, so obtain a mark.

Angles

Simply put, the ability to convert spares lies in choosing the proper angle to shoot from. The angles at which you shoot are based primarily on three pins: the 5, 7, and 10.

The 7. Here your angle will cover all pins to the left on the lane.

The 10. Here your angle will cover all pins to the right of the lane.

The 5. The 5 angle will cover pins located in the center of the lane with the 5 pin as your gauge.

Pin formations that have the head pin standing are bowled from the side opposite the greater number of pins.

With these three angles you should be able to cover pretty much all the spares that will confront you, as a rule of thumb. Simply put, you bowl the left angle from the right, the right angle from the left, and the center from the center.

Let's take a look at bowling these angles.

Bowling 7 pin, 10 pin, and 5 pin leaves. On a 7 pin leave you're postioned to the far right of the lane, using a straight trajectory to your target, crossing over the third arrow. With the 10 pin, you move to the opposite side of the line, using the same trajectory, also crossing the third arrow. With the 5 pin, you bowl the exact line you are using to strike. This is a solid approach to bowling spares, which can be adjusted as you advance in your game.

Now let's look at a few more conversions and the reason for the type of leave. In shooting these spares you may use your strike line with some adjustments to assist you in conversion.

1-2-8. This leave results when the ball doesn't hook up to the pocket, due either to an errant shot or to improper alignment. Move five boards to the right on the approach and throw your ball over your strike line, striking the 1 on the left, the ball carrying into the 2, which takes out the 8.

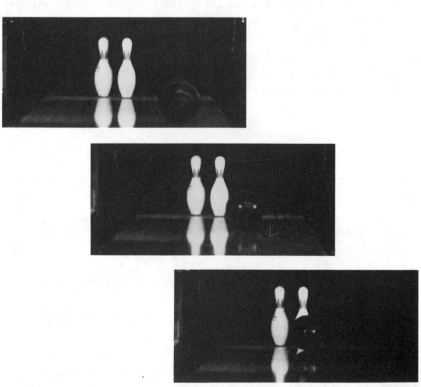

The ball approaches the pocket, strikes between the 1 and 2 pins, taking out the 1, then the 2 . . .

. . . and the 8.

1-2-4-7. This leave results when the ball doesn't hook up to the pocket, being either an errant shot or improper alignment. Move five boards to the right on the approach and throw your ball over your strike line, striking the 1 on the left side, the ball carrying into the 2 pin, with the 2 taking out the 4 and the 4 taking out the 7.

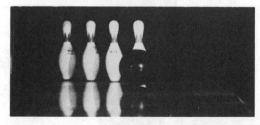

The ball approaches, strikes between the 1 and 2 pins, the 1 and 2 are taken out, . . .

. . . and the 4 and 7 pins follow.

1-3-6-10. This leave is the result of pulling the ball or not properly coming through the ball, which results in the ball hooking early. This is bowled from the strike angle with the ball striking between the 1 and 3, with the 3 taking out the 6 and the 6 the 10.

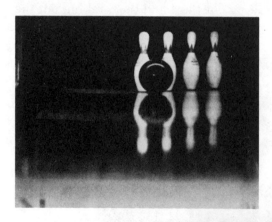

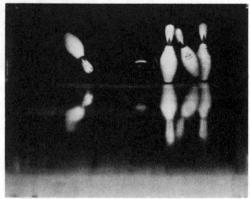

The ball strikes between the 1 and 3 pins and the 3 takes out the 6, with the 6 taking out the 10.

3-6-10. This leave is the result of the ball being set short or being aligned improperly. This is played from the left corner, hitting the 3 on the right side, with your ball taking out the 6 and the 6 taking out the 10.

The ball strikes between the 3 and 6 pins and the 10 is cleared, too.

2-5. This leave results when the ball doesn't hook up to the pocket or because of too much speed or improper alignment. *Initial approach:* This is played from the strike line, moving five boards to the right, allowing your ball to hook between the 2 and 5, hitting the 2 on the right side as your ball takes out the 5. *Optional Approach:* Shooting from the fourth arrow or farther inside, you throw the ball hard and straight to help eliminate chopping the 2 off the 5 pin.

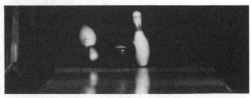

The ball hits between the 2 and 5 pins and take them out.

2-4-5-8. This leave is the result of the ball not hooking up to the pocket, too much speed, or improper alignment. This is played from the strike line, hitting the 2 pin on the right-hand side, with the 2 taking out the 4 and your ball removing the 5 and 8.

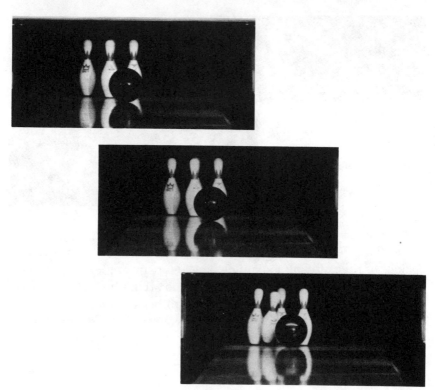

The ball approaches, strikes between the 2 and 5 pins, taking out the 2-5-8, while the 2 clears the 4 out.

These are just a few spares to give you an idea of the 7-10-5 angles.

I think the two most common and toughest spares that you're going to see are the 2-4-5 and the 3-6-10, and once again those are for right-handers.

The 2-4-5 and the 3-6-10 are both very difficult because there are so many ways to miss them. You run the risk of hooking the ball too much on either one of the spares and chopping the 2-4 off the 5 or chopping the 3 off the 6-10 or the 3-6 off the 10. These are probably the two most frequently missed combination spares in the game because they are left so often.

Systems

The world wouldn't be complete without systems, and neither would bowling, which you once thought was a simple game.

The system used in bowling spares involves the 5-8-10 and the 2-4-5.

Let's take the 5-8-10 first. These figures reflect the number of boards you move from your normal position on the lane when you are bowling a strike (my normal position is the second arrow). This adjustment merely alters the angle at which you bowl your ball, much like the 5-7-10 before. The difference is that you don't change your mark, only the boards in relationship to it, always sighting for spares on the left side of the lane. For spares on the right-hand side of the lane your strike line is not used, but you attempt to throw the ball hard and straight, unless you're confronted with the sleeper pin spare, where power is needed to carry through to hit the pin in the back.

Here is a list of the number of boards you must move in the 5-8-10 system.

PINS	BOARDS
1 or 5	Use your strike line
2 or 5	5 boards to right
4	8 boards to right
7	10 boards to right
10	far left across third arrow or deeper
6	2 boards right of 10-pin position
3 or 9	5 boards right of 10-pin position

Just like everything else in bowling, systems cannot meet all the challenges bowling throws at you. So, be careful in using any type of system. The conditions that prevail in all three environments—physical conditions, lane conditions, and pin action—dictate the terms of the game more than anything else. You cannot expect to shoot, for instance, the 7 pin from the right angle on a fully blocked lane coming across the wall and to make it every time. It's particularly important to adjust to the changes on the lanes when making spares. You'll be throwing balls at the full rack setup all night, but the 3-6-10, for example, may come up only once (you hope), and you don't want to blow it because you didn't take the lane condition into consideration.

Everything looks good in theory. When you actually go out and try it, however, you often find out that other variables may exist, and in bowling they surely do.

SPECIAL CONDITIONS

Take into consideration the following variables when bowling spares.

Oily Lanes. If the lanes are oily, your ball is not going to hook a lot, so all you have to do is throw a straight ball to the proper point of the hit to convert the spare.

Blocked Lanes. Here you hit that wall of oil we discussed and your ball fails to hook properly, thus missing its mark. It rides the wall like a barrier and backs off. The only way to overcome this is to aim past your target, compensating for the wall. But be sure to notice the wall from the reaction of your other balls, because if you go cross-lane you will find out too late and miss the spare.

Dry Lanes. Dry lanes give you the reverse situation of the wall or blocked lane. Here the ball will be hooking viciously. The only way to compensate for this condition is to kill your hook, loft the ball, or move to the right side since you will be very limited in your ability to throw a straight ball for the spare.

SPLITS

Most splits are a direct result of hitting too high on the head pin. The problem here is the degree of accuracy that is needed to convert these splits, while taking into consideration the lane conditions, etc. It really becomes *interesting*, for want of a better term.

Like everything else, when this situation occurs it's a red flag, signaling danger, because obviously something's going wrong. So get out your physical checklist to determine what went wrong.

Splits come in varying combinations, some of which are the 5-8-10, 7-10, 8-10, 5-7, 5-10, 4-5-7, and 4-5.

STRATEGY

When bowling difficult splits of the two-pin variety, a bowler is said to "go for the count." Instead of risking all, he takes one pin for the count if the game is close. On the aggressive side, if you're losing by a lot, you might have to "roll the bones" and go for it all.

There are two reasons for opting for the "take the one-pin count" approach over trying for all: (1) the splits' success ratio and (2) pin count.

On splits that are extremely difficult, such as the 4-6, 7-9, 8-10, and 7-10, the only time you're going to try to convert is if you *need* that spare. On the three-pin splits—4-7-10, 6-7-10—you might want to go for two pins instead of risking getting none or just one.

Football is a game of inches; bowling is a game of pins. Sometimes, one or two determine a close match, so you don't want to give up anything without a fight.

MENTAL SCORECARD

You must be able to keep mental score for a very good reason. When the split situation occurs, it's up to you to know if you have to go for the spare or the count, and the only way you're going to know this is by being aware of the score and its potential if your opponent strikes out, etc. If you don't have this mental count, there is no way that you're going to be able to know what to do, and guessing won't be much help. This may seem like an obvious point, but bowlers do sometimes neglect to keep track of the score in the heat of the game. This situation is a reality, and has cost many a game.

CONVERTING SPLITS

Let's now take a look at converting some of the splits that may confront us on the lanes.

4-9

This leave results when the ball comes in slightly high, with the ball finishing strongly, leaving the 9 as the 2 pin goes around the 4.

The ball hits to the left of the 4 pin, driving it into the 9.

This is shot from your strike line, playing to hit the 4 pin on the left side, sending it into the 9. This spare is shot in the same fashion as if you were shooting a 7 pin leave.

3-10

This leave results when the ball comes in high, chopping the 1 off the 3 as the resulting pin action leaves the 10 pin.

Position yourself at the left side of the approach and hit the right side of the 3 pin with your ball, taking the 10 out.

With the 3-10 leave, you need to hit the right side of the 3 pin to drive it into the 10.

4-5

This leave is the result of a light pocket hit and ball deflection.

This split can be shot in the same manner as the 2-5, moving an additional board to the right to fit the ball between the 2 and 5.

The ball strikes between the 4 and 5 pins to clear them.

5-7

This leave is the result of a light pocket hit and deflection off the head pin to the right. To convert the 5-7 when you know there's more oil in the center than on the outside, move three boards to the left on the approach and one board to the left on the lane from your strike line. Position yourself near center and hit the 5 on its right side, driving it into the 7. On dry lanes, use the same adjustment and throw the ball harder.

The ball hits the 5 pin on the right side to drive it across the lane to take out the 7.

Splits occur more often if the lanes are fast, with pins that are heavy.

As we discussed, these heavy pins require a good hit while giving less action. The result will be some extra pins being left to cause more splits, so be alert when the new ABC-sanctioned pins come into play.

TAPS

One of bowling's frustrations is the tap. A tap results when what seemed to be a super shot placed in the pocket comes up with a one-pin leave. Very little consolation can be offered to a competitive bowler who is tapping, especially when his opponent is striking.

You can't totally avoid being tapped. It's simply another fact of the game. Experts say the only real tap in bowling is the solid 8 pin for right-handers and the solid 9 for left-handers and that every other kind of tap, whether it be the 10 pin for the right-handers or the 7 pin for the left-handers, is the result of a less-than-perfect hit.

There are adjustments that can be made, but there are also reasons for leaving those pins. I don't make major adjustments when I'm leaving a lot of solid 10 pins, where the 6 pin is actually flying around the 10 pin (as opposed to the weak 10, where you're hitting a little lighter in the pocket and the 6 pin goes into the gutter and doesn't come out again to hit the 10). On solid taps I don't look to make a big adjustment. I feel that I'm going to get my share of strikes and my share of taps.

I know whenever I go into a new bowling center to bowl with the amateurs on the pro-am event we have every week, the first time I leave a 10 pin, they'll say, "This is really a 10 pin house." I usually come back and tell them, "Well, they all are!" In every bowling center you're going to leave solid 10s. The best way to adjust for leaving a solid 10 is to take your spare ball and pick it up.

Taps are very irritating and can serve as a source of unnecessary frustration to the advanced bowler moving up, but if you're leaving a lot of solid 10s (for the right-handed bowler), you should be fairly pleased with the way you're bowling, because you have to make your shots in order to leave those taps.

You'll see more taps in a professional tournament than you will in any amateur tournament because the bowlers are quality bowlers.

ADJUSTMENTS

Although you're going to leave a certain percentage of taps, there are adjustments that can be made. For example, you can make adjustments in the kind of weight distribution you're using. If you're using a ball that has a positive weight and you're getting tapped a lot, you can go to a ball with negative weight, which will enter the pocket in a little different fashion and might get the 10 pin out. Be aware, though, that you might also start missing the pocket with your adjustment. Instead of leaving 10 pins and getting spares, you might end up leaving splits and getting nothing, so there's a certain element of risk involved.

Converting taps can lead to disaster. As a solid hit becomes a tap, the resulting frustration can block everything else from your mind. Throwing caution to the wind, you then approach the tap haphazardly and miss. Don't lose your cool! Bowl every spare as carefully as you do the first ball. They all count in your score.

Remember, you can learn something even from a bad shot, so all is not lost. Bowlers who can accept adversity and turn it to their benefit will grow quickly in the sport.

There is no substitute for experience in bowling strikes, spares, splits, and taps, but the points are there. They are reflected in your score and the ability to get the job done each and every time you bowl a ball. Each and every time, you should take your best possible shot.

4
BOWLING ERRORS:
THEIR CAUSES AND CORRECTION

In bowling, that short approach to your target can seem like walking a country mile if you ignore some simple rules. Few good bowlers attempt to analyze their game thoroughly enough to secure the knowledge that would make the difference between being a good bowler and being a great one. This unfortunate lack of creativity can hold back any bowler from achieving his full potential.

Let's take a look at some of the frustrating errors that are all but invisible to you but show as glaring marks on your score card. Investing this time will pay dividends in the future, increasing your scores while you enjoy your bowling efforts even more.

This chapter takes a detailed look at errors committed by all bowlers that restrict them from developing a competitive game and the ability to achieve their full potential.

The chapter is divided into three sections that correspond to the sequence of each ball: rolled approach, delivery, and follow-through. Within each section, common areas of error are described in general, then the specific problems and their solutions are listed.

By no means is a complete list of errors included. Our intention is to identify those errors that arise most commonly, to correct them, and to improve your game. By eliminating those errors you can narrow down the problems you have to concentrate on.

I must warn you that self-detection of errors is not all that successful, so a friend who knows bowling or a professional instructor will be a great and objective assistant.

APPROACH

PROPER STANCE

There are so many varying opinions on proper stance that I just don't know if there's an improper starting position. It's a matter of style. For instance, if you looked at the way I start my approach, you might say that it's an improper stance. My stance is quite unorthodox: I start bent over at the waist with the ball hanging down low.

The most important factor in choosing a stance is comfort. If you feel comfortable standing up straight, that's the way you should start. If you feel more comfortable in a lower position, then that might be better for you.

My stance on the approach: as I release the ball (middle) I lose balance, then gain balance (right).

I developed my stance by experimenting. From the standpoint of eliminating certain mistakes, I think adopting a lower position is a good way to start. I would encourage bowlers to give this a try because it eliminates the problems of starting out by standing up straight and then having to gradually move your body position lower to release the ball. You can't release the ball standing straight up; you have to be bent down to a certain degree. As advanced bowlers, you can try a change like this and test the results.

Approach Problem 1: Loss of Balance

Solutions

- Bring the ball closer to your body.
- Distribute your weight evenly.
- Try a higher (erect) or lower ball position and crouch.

PUSHAWAY

You have to have some kind of pushaway to get the ball started unless you start your approach at a higher level, standing straight up so you can let the ball drop down. You don't need a great deal of pushaway, but you still have to get the pushaway started on your first or second step and then continue with your approach, letting the ball swing back and bringing it back through again.

I push the ball away on my first step, and what I actually like to do is get the ball too far ahead of me—I have fast feet that enable me to catch up to the ball and get back into a position for the release.

Technically, this isn't precise. I certainly wouldn't teach anyone to bowl in this fashion. I am able to get the ball back into the right position without having to make drastic adjustments to get my ball and body at the point of release at the right time.

Generally, most bowlers employing a four- or five-step approach push the ball after they've taken a step and continue to make the shot. Whichever you choose, it's a matter of getting yourself into the right position at the foul line, with your body and ball arriving there simultaneously to hit the explosion point.

At left, the ball is too far forward; at right, the proper pushaway is coordinated with the first step.

Approach Problem 2: Improper Pushaway

- not enough swing
- too much swing
- loss of balance during pushaway
- first step goes to left
- ball too far ahead
- timing off
- shoulder injury

Solutions

- Support your ball with your other hand.
- Don't drop the ball down.
- Push ball out straight.
- Keep your elbow at your hip on the ball side.
- Push away on the first step.
- Straighten your arm by locking your elbow.
- Do not lunge forward with the ball.
- Do not drop the ball suddenly.
- Try pushing away earlier.

I sway as I start my approach and sway further as I complete my first right-foot step.

BALL CARRY

You want to be free, not rigid, in the way you carry the ball. Start it off into your backswing and let it flow freely.

From the front, you can see my approach is straight with my eyes fixed on target.

As I release the ball, my weight is off to the right, causing my left foot to hop to maintain balance.

Approach Problem 3:
Zig-zag Walk—Drifting

Solutions

- Don't let ball drop at pushaway.
- Keep shoulders square.
- Walk straight.
- Keep ball alongside.
- Compare the boards you start on and finish on.
- Slow down and look straight ahead.

HOP

I've seen a few amateur bowlers hop, and it's usually at the point of release. When you do this you lose all your power. You also lose leverage in the slide when you hop, and your ball will be very weak and bounce off the pins.

Approach Problem 4:
Hopping

Solutions

- Walk slower
- Accentuate slide.
- Walk straight.
- Keep the ball close to your body.

As I approach the foul line, my left knee is bent. As I release the ball my right foot goes up and I slide. The ball is on its way and my right leg comes down.

HESITATION

Henry Gonzales incorporates a hesitation step into his approach; it's part of his personal style. I believe he calls it a *timing step*, and he actually comes to a stop in the middle of his approach. This is something that I wouldn't recommend that you use in your game. It's very natural to Henry—in fact, it would be difficult for him to try to stop doing this—but for most bowlers it will cause problems.

Approach Problem 5: Hesitation

Solutions

- Coordinate your steps with your arm swing.
- Reduce your backswing.
- Relax.
- Move smoothly.
- Practice your approach without the ball.

This hesitation step will cause most bowlers problems.

COORDINATION

If you are involved in the game of bowling and you've reached a level where you're close to being a competitive bowler, I wouldn't think that coordination would be that big a problem. Some people have a natural sense of timing for the game. However, a lack of timing will affect the effective execution of movement.

Approach Problem 6:
Timing Off

Solutions

- Eliminate hesitation.
- Slow down your approach.
- Speed up your approach.
- Reduce your backswing.
- Relax.
- Push away on the first step.
- Don't force the forward swing.
- Count your steps to yourself.

The ball is too far forward, ahead of my feet—a timing problem.

ALIGNMENT

Some bowlers have trouble with their alignment. Instead of being square with the line when they start their approach, they start with their shoulders "open."

A young bowler on tour, Mike Steinback, looks as if he may be on lane 1, but his shoulders look like they're pointing to lane 4. He's really got himself open to a great degree. Bowling in this fashion allows him to deliver the ball with an inside-out swing, pushing off to the right and swinging the ball out at the same time.

When he has to go straighter, he then has to pull the ball straighter. I think it's an advantage to be a little more square up the line. The only time you really want to change your alignment is when you're playing deep inside. Then you may want to open your shoulders up a little bit; however, if you have to play the second arrow, it's very difficult to do so with your shoulders aligned in that manner.

Approach Problem 7: Improper Alignment

- pendulum swing not straight
- loss of accuracy

Solutions:

- Square shoulders to the line.
- Bend your left knee on release.
- Practice without the ball.
- Slow down.
- Maintain your balance.

At left, my shoulders aren't "squared" and thus my shot won't be aligned properly. At right is the correct position for proper alignment.

With proper alignment, I can loft the ball over the foul line and my follow-through leaves me balanced.

GRIPS

Everybody has problems with grips. I have problems with grips, and I've been bowling for 20 years. You have to experiment with your grip and find somebody with whom you're comfortable to drill your equipment. Keep trying small adjustments to find the ulitmate grip.

Grips are very personal. I was lucky in finding mine, even though I do still have small problems with the way the ball feels. I've always said that if I could have a good feel of the ball all the time, with the ball feeling like an extension of my body, I could win twice as much as I win now. I know that every bowler feels the same way. There aren't that many bowlers who are comfortable with their grip.

My problem is that my hand never stays the same size. It constantly swells and shrinks, making it almost impossible to get a good consistent feel of the ball.

I don't often feel like I have a really good grip, but I've learned to live with this by trying some of the solutions below.

Approach Problem 8: Poor Grip

- uncomfortable grip
- dropping the ball

Solutions

- Check span of fingers.
- Adjust grip to conventional, semifingertip (recommended), or fingertip.
- See a ball fitter.
- Use inserts.

DRIFTING

The way a bowler approaches the line often dictates that, starting out on a given spot on the approach, he will move to the right or the left as he walks up the approach.

If you're a right-hander, it's more advantageous to drift to the left than to the right. If you drift to the right, it's very difficult to get any power. If you drift to the left, your shoulders tend to open up a little bit, and you can impart the inside-out swing and get the lift and power out of the ball that you need. You don't want to exaggerate the drift too much, although there are exceptions to every rule.

Ted Hannahs, who is an extremely good bowler, one of the best we have on tour today, drifts approximately 15–20 boards on the approach on all of his shots. I drift about 5 boards, which is an acceptable number, but for Ted 20 boards is acceptable.

Approach Problem 9:
Drifting

Solutions

- Keep it to a minimum.
- Adjust to your game.
- Slow down and count your steps.

BEING AGGRESSIVE WITH YOUR FEET

I have fast feet to begin with, and when I get excited I have a tendency to become even faster, losing my ability to control the ball. Sometimes I have to concentrate on keeping my feet moving a little slower.

Approach Problem 10:
Feet Ahead of Ball

Solutions

- Slow down.
- Count your steps.
- Don't carry the ball.

DELIVERY

FORCED SWING FORWARD

You never want to force the swing. You should incorporate it into your approach. You must develop a smooth swing so that you don't have to force it through.

If you're forcing the swing through, you probably are getting yourself ahead of the ball to the point where your body is out of position to release the ball. Your arm swing has not come down because your arm hasn't come through. If you pull the ball through, you're going to be making an errant shot.

Delivery Problem 1:
Forcing the Swing Forward

- dropping the ball
- loss of loft

Solutions

- Check timing.
- Coordinate arm swing and steps.
- Reduce exaggerated force to the ball.
- Reduce backswing.
- Don't carry the ball.
- Allow the ball to swing freely.
- Increase time before release.

At left, my feet are too far ahead of the ball. At right, my timing is correct and my feet are coordinated with the movement of the ball.

BALANCE

I maintain my balance by counterbalancing myself with my left hand. If I were to keep my left arm totally out of the shot by keeping it next to my body, there would be no way I could counteract the effects of a 16-pound bowling ball coming through next to my body. My left arm must be out to counterbalance myself. All bowlers do this.

Delivery Problem 2: Loss of Balance

Solutions

- Counterbalance with your left hand.
- Remain square.
- Relax.
- Slow down.

At left, my left arm is too close to my side, causing an imbalance to my shot. At right, my arms are in proper coordination.

DROPPING THE BALL

Only one bowler I know of has had any success with dropping the ball early, and that is Larry Laub. Larry has been successful for many years by starting the ball out right at the foul line or sometimes behind the foul line. He's the only one I can think of who uses this technique.

If you have a problem with dropping the ball, it may be that the ball is too heavy for you or you're not using the proper grip. Your thumb hole might be a little loose, or your finger holes might be loose.

You might need to go with tightening the holes up, which can be done by using cork inserts or electrician's or adhesive tape. These things will take up the slack in the holes.

Delivery Problem 3:
Dropping the Ball

Solutions

- Use inserts when holes are too big.
- Use lighter ball if ball is too heavy.
- Experiment with different grips.

At left, I dropped the ball before the line. At right, the ball is lofted over the line properly.

SLIDE COORDINATION

I take a long slide—about two feet long—that gives me the control I need. Most bowlers don't take a slide quite as long as mine. In fact, some bowlers hardly take a slide at all; they go into the motions, but they actually plant their left foot (for right-handers) and pull the ball through. I think this happens because it's the easiest way for bowlers to create the kind of leverage and power they need on the ball. However, I feel that you do need to have some type of slide in order to keep your balance at the line.

Delivery Problem 4: Loss of Balance during Delivery

Solutions

- Slow down approach.
- Lengthen slide.
- Purchase proper shoes.
- Take shorter steps.
- Bend knee of sliding leg.
- Face your line squarely.

FOLLOW-THROUGH

FOULING

If you're having problems fouling, you may have to move back on the approach, or you might be having trouble with approaches being a little slippery or tacky. Unfortunately, that happens sometimes.

When the approaches aren't quite to your liking, you can make adjustments with the sole of your slide shoe. You can apply something that will allow you to slide a little more or, if conditions are really slippery, go with something that would stop you a little sooner.

A shoe is available that allows you to change the sole. It comes with little round inserts: the leather gives you a normal approach; the rubber inserts make you stop; the Teflon enables you to slide more.

Follow-Through Problem 1: Fouling

Solutions

- Check lane conditions and use proper sole to meet condition (slippery or tacky).
- Lengthen approach.
- Slow down.

My left foot slides too far, causing a foul.

TOO MUCH OR TOO LITTLE FOLLOW-THROUGH

You can definitely follow through too much, but I feel that it's more common for bowlers to follow through too little. We call this *setting the ball short*. The ball will start rolling too early, not giving it a chance to skid, roll, and hook. The ball has to skid a certain number of feet, then roll and hook to be effective, and the amount of follow-through can affect this dramatically.

Follow-Through Problem 2: Too Little

- no lift
- dropping the ball

Solutions

- Keep your wrist straight.
- Use a wrist device.
- Follow your mark.
- Slow down.
- Follow through totally— don't stop swing of arm.
- Check your release.

Too little follow-through in both examples.

Follow-Through Problem 3: Too Much

- lofting ball
- loss of balance

Solutions

- Reduce arm swing.
- Check tightness of ball holes, allowing the release of your fingers.
- Slow down.
- Relax.
- Don't exaggerate power.
- Reduce lift.
- Bend sliding leg at knee.

The proper amount of follow-through.

IMPROPER RELEASE

Most bowlers who are trying to impart hook to the ball think it's done with side roll, but it's the forward roll that gives the power, with a little bit of side roll causing your ball to break from right to left (for right-handers) or left to right (for left-handers). It is here that the confusion starts that causes bowlers to invent all types of exaggerated releases to achieve their desired results.

I think a lot of bowlers would be surprised to know where the track is on my ball, because it is not as low as it looks. It's a fairly high track, near the thumb hole, because I apply a great deal of forward roll to it.

Follow-Through Problem 4: Improper Release

Solutions

- Reduce side roll.
- Stay behind the ball.
- Check grips.
- Use inserts.
- Slow down.

Improper release, left; proper release, right.

GENERAL PROBLEMS

The following deals with general problems and their possible solutions.

Too Much Speed

Solutions

- Relax.
- Reduce backswing and pushaway.
- Slow down.
- Develop your feel for speed, its need, its control.

Ball Deflects

Solutions

- Follow through more.
- Stay behind the ball.
- Impart lift and forward roll.

The list can go on forever, but the problems covered above give you a good idea of how to approach any trouble areas you identify. These errors are costly to both your score and your enjoyment.

Spend some time working on your weaknesses, using the problem/solution approach. It will help you evaluate your game.

MARSHALL HOLMAN BOWLING PERFORMANCE ANALYZER

Since bowling has so many variables to consider in evaluating your game and making the necessary adjustments, it may be good to sit down and use the Marshall Holman Bowling Performance Analyzer.

The analyzer illustrated on page 93 forms a relationship between the positive and negative forces in your game. In order to derive the full potential from the analyzer you must be honest with yourself when analyzing your game.

Above the present performance line, list all those negative things that you feel are holding you back from attaining the skills necessary to reach the optimum performance line.

MARSHALL HOLMAN BOWLING PERFORMANCE ANALYZER: AN EXAMPLE

----

poor attitude	**OPTIMUM**
lack of concentration	**PERFORMANCE**
drifting	**LEVEL**
cannot identify lane conditions	
inconsistent approach	**NEGATIVE FORCES**
poor line adjustment	**45%**
lane adjustment poor	
nervous (mental game poor)	
too many conversions	

good ball speed	**PRESENT**
good ball roll	**PREFORMANCE**
good release	**LEVEL**
good followthrough	
good hand positions	**POSITIVE FORCES**
proper choice of ball	**55%**
good pin aciton	
understand splits	
understand spares	
proper equipment maintenance	
good knowledge of scoring	

FIELDS OF FORCES FOR PERFORMANCE ANALYZER

Physical Game: Stance, Approach, Release, Follow-through, Release, Ball
    Roll, Ball Speed
Pin Action: Ability to understand, Ability to adjust
Lane Conditions: Ability to identify, Ability to adjust
Spares, Splits, Taps: Conversions, Adjustments
Mental Game: Concentration, Attitude, Ability to adjust, Preparation, Strategy,
    Pacing, Personality on lanes, Time management, Financial
    management, Intimidation
Physical Condition: Proper diet, Sufficient rest, Proper exercise, Endurance,
    Injury-prone, Sufficient practice, Adequate warm-up

Below the present performance line, list all those positive things
in your game that are pushing you toward the level you wish to
reach. The optimum level here is your desired level of performance, which may be to become a better league bowler or to
become a professional on tour.

Whatever your aspirations, the Marshall Holman Bowling Performance Analyzer will allow you to determine your position in the field of forces illustrated below while analyzing the negative and positive forces in order to make the necessary changes to reach your optimum level of performance.

After listing the positive forces that are raising your present level of performance and the negative forces holding you back from achieving full potential, add them up and divide 100 by the total number of entries. For example, if you have a total of 20 listings, give each a weight of 5. With 100 percent representing the optimum level, you can evaluate your overall effectiveness. In the Illus. given, 9 areas (or 45 percent) of the performance are negative. Therefore, the remaining 11 areas (or 55 percent) are positive. The bowler in question is far below achieving his full potential and must reduce the areas on the negative side of the chart to increase his overall effectiveness.

For the bowler in our example, there is ample information in this book to help him eliminate the nine negative forces that prevent him from achieving optimum performance. Text beginning on page 138 addresses how to develop a positive attitude, and later, on page 142, concentration is discussed. Later yet in that chapter (page 145) nervousness and the mental game are covered. Chapter 3 addresses conversion problems in great detail. The remaining problems are all discussed as follows:

> *Drifting*—page 83.
> *Identifying lane conditions*—page 99.
> *Approach problems*—page 73.
> *Line adjustments*—page 81.
> *Lane adjustments*—page 116.

By concentrating on your weak areas and eliminating them, you will increase you positive forces while approaching your optimum performance level. You can update the performance analyzer as you reach different stages of development. By using this approach, you can compile an overall average at the beginning and track each interval of movement up or down. The differential in average will serve as an indicator of your overall progress both on the analyzer and on the lanes.

5
LANE CONDITIONS

That magical piece of real estate separating the bowler from the pins controls the outcome of the game more than some bowlers realize or care to admit. With today's concern for ensuring the protection and competitiveness of the lanes, the bowler must be increasingly aware of how to analyze these situations.

This is by no means an easy task, and one reason is the dearth of information on the subject.

Let's uncover a partially undiscovered treasure, the ability to read and play lane conditions, the bounty of which is the key to greater success on the lanes.

A MOST DIFFICULT OPPONENT

Lane conditions are one of the most complicated aspects of the game and one of the least understood by most bowlers. The power they exert over the game is what holds back most bowlers from a competitive game. The professional bowler has by no means escaped this situation, as you see on the weekly PBA Tour telecast.

The top bowlers in the world will attempt to adjust their game to suit the lane condition that prevails and sometimes still not find the answer.

To appreciate fully what we are dealing with, I feel it is essential to take a look at the lanes to obtain an intimate knowledge of what is actually out there.

Lane conditions refers to the condition of the lanes resulting from their maintenance. Lane conditions vary from bowling center to bowling center and can even differ in respect to "climactic" changes on the same lane. The difference between a lane's reaction early in the day and its reaction later in the evening is like night and day, pardon the pun.

Lanes are made of wood or a synthetic, which expand and contract due to certain temperature changes. Wood consists mostly of cellulose and lignin. When a lane is initially constructed, it is the intention of the builder that it be entirely flat.

The surface or top of the lane is usually finished with urethane, much like kitchen cabinets or other fine wood products, to protect it. After application of the finish, an oil is added to cover the surface. When this preparation is applied, the lane is considered *dressed*.

The constant path of bowling balls traveling on this surface removes the oil and finish, and the lanes can get down to the bare wood in some areas. Obviously, this is a most undesirable situation, since the exposed lane is then subject to direct contact with the ball and permanent damage. If this condition is allowed to continue, the lane will deteriorate and become uneven. Correspondingly, these variations in level or other inconsistencies in pitch can be a disaster to one's game, affecting roll, path, and much more.

If maintained properly, the lanes will not be damaged but will be in a constant state of dressing. Oil is applied daily, and the way in which it's applied, the amount that is applied, etc., will all affect your game. The actual finish lasts a couple of months, depending on the traffic.

Of course, some lanes are dressed better than others. The critical factor, however, comes into play when dropped balls or normal wear and tear create indentations in the lanes.

When a lane is allowed to get into less-than-perfect condition, even when it's resurfaced, the liquids used will seek their own levels and become applied unevenly, no matter what corrective measures are taken.

TYPES OF LANES

Lanes, like bowlers, acquire certain characteristics and personalities with use. General types of lanes are described below.

FLAT

The perfectly flat lane is obviously the most desirable. In reading its surface you can forget about inconsistencies in structure and deal instead with oil, etc.

CROWNED

When lanes become crowned, they give the appearance somewhat of an inverted V, being higher in the middle. This condition increases scoring, because the ball is prevented from crossing over and away from the 17th board by the raised (or crowned) condition.

This is not a competitive condition (where lanes oppose you), but rather a high-scoring one that gets worse with the application of oils. It is caused by the method of resurfacing and the intentional cutting down of the outside areas of the lanes to create the crown and a high-scoring condition.

DISHED

Exactly as it sounds, a dished lane is beveled down the middle and again creates a condition that's less than desirable. It appears similar to a V shape, but the trough running down the center of the lane is not as pronounced.

WHAT ACTUALLY CAUSES LANE CONDITIONS

Remember, the lanes are made of wood, which has grains or textures that make up its surface. The finish is applied to the lanes for the purpose of sealing the wood and protecting it. As the finish is worn, the open wood grains become exposed to the ball. When oil is applied to an open-grained area, it is absorbed by the bare wood due to the absence of finish. This creates a dried area, where other areas may be wet and oily. Add to this the fact that the lanes are made of different woods (maple/pine/maple), and you have a situation rife with problems.

Sometimes the lanes will appear blotchy when highlighted by the bowling center's lighting. This indicates the dry and oily conditions we've discussed.

Oil actually holds your ball in play, but its tendency to evaporate during the course of a tournament makes the environment on the lane change. You'll find yourself having to adjust once the oil stops holding your ball in play.

No environmental factor is affected more than your ball. If you recall, when discussing bowling balls we said the ball picks up the oil from the lanes. This also changes your environment, and the excess oil must be removed from your ball after each roll.

Oil can be applied to lanes manually or by machine. I prefer the manually applied method since the oil is actually rubbed into the lanes, allowing it to penetrate and to distribute more evenly. In machine application, the oil sometimes sits on top of the lanes and collects at the level of lane imperfections.

When properly applied to the lanes, oil ensures that the ball will slide the first 20 feet, then roll the next 20, and hook the last 20 feet.

Conditions on lanes vary from dry, to spotty, to wet, and every combination in between. For now, let's get into some general aspects before discussing several technical terms that describe various conditions.

BEFORE YOU BLAME THE LANES

It may sound oversimplified, but I watch what other players are doing before I jump to any conclusions about the lanes. If I find myself struggling, and I see players with games similar to my own who are doing well, then I don't think I have the right to blame the lane conditions.

If you notice this situation, you then have to look to whether you're making good shots or whether you're using the right equipment for that lane condition.

It's easy for bowlers to use the lane condition as an excuse for bowling a poor physical game. Bowling a poor game happens frequently, whatever your level. The 175-average league bowlers are still affected by lane conditions. But whatever your level, the cop-out is always available; you can always blame it on the lanes. If you're bowling for a living, however, there comes a time when you have to forget about blaming the lanes and concentrate on ways to make yourself effective, regardless of lane conditions.

ESTABLISH A CHECKLIST

The most effective way to do this is to establish a checklist to evaluate your physical game first and then, if necessary, move on to the lane conditions that exist.

You could check to see if you're following through toward your target. This means not only with your hand, but also with the inside of your right elbow (for right-handers) or with the inside of your left elbow (for left-handers). This will keep your arm straight toward the target and also keep your hand behind the ball. If you follow through toward the target but don't keep your elbow or your hand behind the ball, you're not doing any good at all.

Make sure that you are mentally aware of what you're doing and that you're concentrating on your mark. You can even exaggerate your concentration so that you're not just looking at the mark, throwing the ball, watching your spot, and watching your ball hit the pins. You might watch the ball pass the mark you're using (most bowlers use the arrows that are 15–20 feet down the lane) for an extra 10 feet before you look up.

Keep your body down through the shot and do not "come off the shot," as the pros say, which will make you overanxious at release. It's like keeping your eye on the ball in golf when you're hitting the ball and waiting for your follow-through to take your eyes off the ball. Once you've determined that you're following through and that your physical game is on cue, you can start to adjust your positioning to counteract the lane conditions that exist.

IDENTIFYING, AND ADJUSTING TO, LANE CONDITIONS

You have to sense a lane condition; you can't go out and feel it with your hand or see it with your eyes. As mentioned earlier, you can see blotchy conditions highlighted on the lanes, but this is not what I mean, for this is only a reflection of light that tells you nothing useful.

No matter what your level of playing ability is, if you're trying to combat lane conditions, all you can do is make your best shot and watch the way your ball reacts to the lanes. This is one way to detect what is happening—by the way your ball reacts to the lanes.

Generally, whether you're right- or left-handed, start playing at right about the second arrow or the 10th board.

First you have to be warmed up. Then throw a couple of practice shots. If the ball is hooking too much from that particular line, it's a good idea to move two boards to the left on the approach and a board on the lane, since there's generally more lane conditioning or more oil on the inside of the lane than there is on the outside. You can keep making these small adjustments until you reach an advantageous position on the lane.

If you try this and the ball slides, you can move out on the lane by moving out a board on the lane and out two boards on the approach and continue to make small adjustments until you get lined up.

Now, if that approach just isn't working, and you feel that there's more oil on the outside of the lane (your previous adjustments were made with the thought that the oil was greater inside), then there are a few different ways to make adjustments.

If you're a bowler like Ernie Schlegel, you might move out a little bit and just try to keep the ball in the pocket all the way and not try to overhook it. Just throw the ball straight at the pocket and watch the results of your straight ball.

If you hook the ball more, like I do, and the situation presented is the same, with the condition being dry in the middle and wet on the outside, you can go with a harder-surfaced ball. Just play farther inside and throw the ball. Now you have the harder surface of the ball in addition to more ball speed.

WEIGHT DISTRIBUTION

Many different adjustments can be made. Weight distribution in the ball is one example.

By using more positive weight, you can stop the ball from hooking too soon.

If the condition of the lanes is such that they are dry on the inside and oily on the outside, and your problem is that your ball keeps driving on to the head pin too fully, causing splits, not even coming close to a strike, you've got to be aggressive enough to make the kind of adjustments that are necessary without hesitating or doubting your judgment.

If you're using a softer-shell ball, which most bowlers use, it's important to have a harder-shell ball with you. If you're going to have only two balls with you, one of them must have a harder shell to combat the drier lane conditions that may arise as the day goes on.

TRACK SHOTS

This type of shot comes into play more for right-handers than for left-handers, because there really aren't enough left-handers to build in a sufficient track on the left side of the lane.

The track shot is where you have to keep your ball in the track, no matter what kind of lane procedure is done on it unless it's very drastic and alters the track. The alternatives here are minimal, but identifying the condition is of paramount importance.

A good example of track shot conditions is in Toledo at Imperial Lanes, where for years the track has been *very* dominant. No matter what they do to the lanes, you have to have your ball between the second and third arrows. If it gets outside the second arrow, it just won't bite because it gets by the track.

This is indicative of the conditions we discussed in the beginning of the chapter, when a situation is created in a lane that is difficult, if not impossible (as in the track), to remove or correct without completely replacing the alley.

In the track shot, you have to stay within the track. If you throw the ball with a lot of hook and you're in a track shot type of condition, you've got to go with the harder-shell ball and just make sure you keep it in the track, not swinging the ball too far to the right.

That's where a lot of the young players who come on tour are at a disadvantage. We get that type of condition rarely, but we've seen it. They have to be aware of it and be able to combat it. The younger players attempt to move far inside the lane and throw the ball to the right, bringing it back. You can't make it come back, no matter how much power you put on the ball; the lane will be too dominant over your ball. So you have to do what the lane condition allows you to do.

It's important to understand that, when combating lane conditions, you can't try to make something out of a condition that isn't there.

BACK ENDS HOOK

When the back ends are hooking a lot you can throw the ball to the right if you're right-handed or to the left if you're left-handed and be pretty well assured that your ball is going to hook back to the pocket. With that kind of condition, it's advantageous to use a softer-shell ball to give yourself even more area in which to get the ball back to the pocket.

I feel the oil condition will affect the hooking on the back end condition more than it will the tracking. If there's not as much oil in the track condition, you're going to have to go with the harder ball. If there is a lot of oil, go with the softer ball. You make pretty much the same general adjustments under the condition of hooking back ends. There's a good deal more room for error, and this is generally a higher-scoring condition.

BLOCKED LANES

When the oil is on the outside and the dry boards are on the inside, the lane is blocked. Here, you're going to have higher scores, but there's more margin for error. The conditions of the lanes can easily be manipulated in the game of bowling. It's like playing on a long par-5 golf hole without much fairway to work with. You've got to do the best you can with it. I'll discuss adjustments for a variety of blocked conditions later in this chapter.

LOW SCORES

You're definitely not going to score as high when the lanes have oil on the outside and dry boards around the inside. On the pro tour this sometimes comes into play, especially late in the afternoon or evening during a tournament, because the lanes are oiled only once a day, before the competition starts.

That's where having a number of different bowling balls comes into play. I think that, if you took the average number of bowling balls the professionals take along and have at their disposal at any one time, it would probably be well over eight.

As we have said, when the oil is on the inside and the outside is dry, the condition is called a *block*. The block gives you very high scores. It allows you to have the range as far as your accuracy is concerned, since you can throw the ball too far to the right (for right-handers) and still get it back because the lane is dry on the outside, bringing the ball back into the pocket. You could throw the ball to the left, and the amount of lane conditioner on the lane (if done properly) will hold the ball all the way toward the pins.

On one shot your ball could hook 15 boards and strike, and you could come back on the same lane for your next shot and hook only three boards and strike, depending on whether you've pulled one or thrown one too far to the right.

I would suggest you use a soft urethane ball when there's a good deal of oil in the middle and dryness on the outside, because that ball will increase the area you will be able to use.

When the oil is on the outside and it's dry on the inside, I would take a hard plastic ball and play pretty much in the dry area.

For me, it's easier to combat the dry areas than it would be to try to go into the wet area and make the ball hook back to the pocket. That's almost impossible.

THE DEEP INSIDE SHOT

This is the shot called for when the only way to play the lane is to play inside the fourth arrow. Not many amateurs find themselves forced to play that kind of shot.

What you do here is try to cut down your hook and just try to keep the ball in the pocket all the way. You could also use what's called the *fall-back shot* (described in Chapter 2), where you're playing inside the 17th board and you're letting the ball actually back into the pocket instead of hooking it into the pocket. In this case, the ball isn't hooking the last 10 feet at all, but it's either going straight or actually going a little bit to the right.

This condition is caused by the lane getting dry and unplayable on the outside of the lane, causing you to move in. There's sufficient oil in the middle of the lane so that your ball won't hook early, but you don't have the back ends hooking.

When the lane is really dry inside and really wet on the outside

The gutter shot in all its glory, taking advantage of the wet conditions on the outside and avoiding the dry inside lane.

you might move all the way out to the one, two, or three board, which we call the *gutter shot*. At times that becomes a playable area, and that's also like the shot from deep inside; the extreme outside shot is not used very often by amateur bowlers or a bowler who is not bowling a lot.

EQUIPMENT FOR MAKING ADJUSTMENTS

In choosing the right ball for these conditions, you have to go by what your own game is, and what's going to work for me isn't necessarily going to work for everyone else. What's going to work is a personal and individual matter.

You can make adjustments with the equipment by going to a harder or softer ball. You can also make adjustments to where the lane is hooking all over with hand positions by the way that you come out of the ball.

There are also many types of wrist supports and other gear that you can use to reach certain goals. Most of the wrist supports are made to give you a more powerful ball and keep your wrist in a strong position, for that's where the main source of the power is on your ball. People think lift with your fingers is what gives you the strike power going into the pocket, but it's actually the power that's imparted by your wrist.

I have used wrist supports on occasion, but I don't feel they're really necessary for my kind of game, since I have a natural release that keeps my wrist in that strong position.

There's even a device that can be used to keep your elbow in position and keep it from chicken-winging the ball. Appropriately, it's called a *chicken wing eliminator*. I'm not a strong advocate of it, but some players do use it to keep them behind the ball.

BALL ROLL

If you impart a lot of side roll or you go with more forward roll when the lanes are really dry—even when using a harder ball—there are times when just the harder ball is not enough to cut down the hook. You have to go with extra speed and try to kill the roll.

You can control ball roll to combat all lane conditions. You might be able to hit the pocket, but you may need to impart a little different kind of roll in order to carry the pins properly.

HAND POSITIONS

The pros use the hand as if it were a clock to determine hand positions. You can start with the thumb at the position I use, at

At left, the 3 o'clock position; at right, the 12 o'clock position.

about three o'clock, and then come around the ball to impart a lot of side roll and forward roll.

If the lanes are hooking more, you can rotate your hand a little more toward 12 o'clock, and then you don't have to rotate your hand as far around the ball, so you will come out with a straighter roll.

I personally don't change my hand position this way. I'm more of an instinctive player, and when I want to adjust how I'm rolling the ball, I make at-the-line adjustments.

ADJUSTMENTS AT THE LINE

I always start with the same hand position, but I can always make the adjustments at the point of release to get more forward roll. A player like Pete Couture will actually start at many different hand positions to impart many different types of roll.

I'll do the same thing with at-the-line corrections.

STEP ADJUSTMENTS

I would not use step adjustment in my approach to combat lane conditions, but some bowlers do. Mike Durbin, an extremely talented bowler who has won tournaments with three, four, and five steps, is the only bowler I've ever known to do that.

Changing the number of steps in my approach just isn't part of my game. I'm able to make the adjustments that are necessary without actually changing the look of my game. I wouldn't really suggest that people who are used to taking a four-step approach switch to three or five steps. I would be more apt to suggest going between four and five than between three and four or three and five. It's just difficult to do.

Some bowlers, like Mark Roth, take either six or seven steps. It seems Mark does it just as the mood suits him. He's a very instinctive player, he knows whether it is necessary to take more or fewer steps. I don't know if he could explain to you why he really does it, but he is very seldom wrong about his adjustments.

ARM SWING

This is one adjustment I can't see anyone making to meet lane conditions. The arm swing should be a simple motion that lets the arm go straight up and straight back. You push the ball away and it comes straight back along the pendulum line and follows right back and through again. I would never consciously try to alter that natural path.

HAND GRIP

Steve Fehr uses a grip involving his middle and ring fingers. He has another hole in the ball for his index finger. This grip helps keep him behind the ball better. He's perfected his game this way, but I would have a hard time doing this.

As you've seen so far, the possibilities involved in combating lane conditions are numerous, with adjustments being made physically and with equipment to make the proper modifications. You'll find that you can make adjustments through an entire match without finding the proper combination. Therefore, you must be able to identify readily certain conditions that occur and make the corresponding adjustments.

HOW TO HANDLE SPECIFIC LANE CONDITIONS

The following are specific conditions you're likely to encounter, with tips on equipment and physical adjustments that can help you adapt to them.

THE FULL BLOCK

Here the outside of the lane is dry and the inside wet. The oil on the inside actually forms a wall to the pocket, which can result in high scores.

Type of ball: soft to moderate urethane
Physical adjustments: none
Other considerations: Find the oil line, so if you pull the ball it will hold the line and if you swing the ball it will hook back to the pocket.

FEATHERED BLOCK

The feathered block occurs when more oil is in the middle, but there is still some oil on the outside of the lane. This is a condition most pros like to see because they can score fairly well on it, but it still demands good shot making.

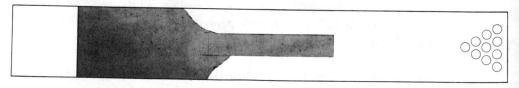

Type of ball: soft to moderate urethane
Physical adjustments: none
Other considerations: This condition is much like the full block, but the large margin for error is reduced so that better shot making is required.

BLOCKED LANE FOR A RIGHT-HANDER

Since there are, as we've said, many more right-handed than left-handed bowlers, the right side of the lane will become tracked by removal of the oil from constant bowling. The heavy concentration of oil on the left side creates a restriction for the right-handed bowler.

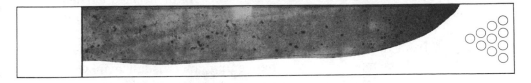

Type of ball: soft to moderate urethane
Physical adjustments: none

PROPERLY OILED LANE

Before we identify other conditions, let's take a look at a properly oiled lane to see what happens. The properly oiled lane, for the purposes of illustration should look something like the figure below.

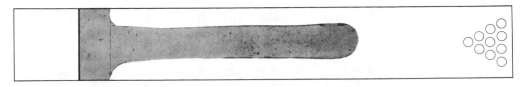

An even texture is maintained throughout, favoring neither the left-handed nor the right-handed bowler at the start. But, as bowling balls are thrown on the lanes, they skid, roll, and hook, changing the initial oil conditions. Even if good maintenance has prevented buildups or bevels in the lane surface, normal lane use will result in a variety of less-than-optimum conditions.

Oil is a liquid and, like water, seeks its own level on a flat or an uneven surface. This creates higher concentrations in some areas than in others so that the properly oiled lane that we saw above now looks like the figure on page 110 from the very start:

The spotty oil concentration shown is exaggerated to give you an idea of the inconsistency you'll encounter. As mentioned earlier, you won't really be able to see this condition. You'll be standing some 60 feet down the line, and you really won't know what to expect from the lane. So you must quickly determine from your practice shots exactly what's happening and visualize in your mind the lane condition that exists so you can quickly make the proper adjustments.

Let's assume you've thrown some practice balls. The figure below illustrates the tracks made from those practice balls, again exaggerated to emphasize the change that is taking place.

Clearly, the marks left by the ball's path to the pins has removed varying amounts of oil from the lane surface, changing the condition that existed at the start.

At this point you also have to take into account the porosity of your bowling ball's surface. Because it's porous, your ball will pick up oil from the lanes, resulting in less oil on the lanes. If you don't wipe the oil off your ball after each roll, as I do, you can imagine the adverse effect it will have on the outcome of your shot as it hits heavily oiled, lightly oiled, or dry surfaces. It's like someone changing gears constantly without a knowledge of what he or she is doing. The result obviously is not a smooth trip.

Again, it's sometimes the little things like this that make a difference in your game. You must be a thinking bowler, constantly aware of these slight changes that can mean extra pins and often the difference between winning and losing.

The ball you're throwing, as we said, should skid, roll, and hook. This concept illustrated on page 111, with the lane divided to represent an approximation of where these events should take place—they have a significant bearing on your shot and the lane.

Skid 20 feet   Roll 40 feet   Hook

This path of the ball's roll obviously affects the distribution of the oil on the lane. Let's take a look at a hypothetical situation, again somewhat exaggerated to illustrate the effect on lane conditions.

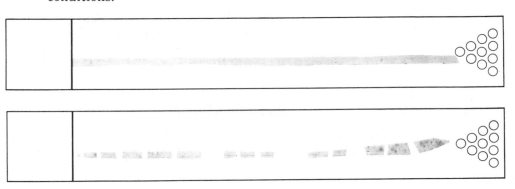

The ball has had an obvious effect on the distribution of the oil. The roll picked up more oil than the skid, and the hook's divergent path removed only portions of oil where it touched.

The next bowler will now be faced with a totally different condition from that faced by the first. Talk about challenges! This is what makes bowling fun.

REVERSE BLOCK

As the name of this condition implies, the reverse block is the opposite of the block: the lane is oily on the outside and dry in the middle. This situation creates potentially low-scoring conditions and demands greater adjustments.

Just the description of this condition indicates that something is wrong. Why no oil in the middle? Obviously, the lane hasn't been oiled, which does happen occasionally. A missed day of oiling will create this condition.

This condition is illustrated on page 112.

Type of ball: hard urethane or soft/hard polyester

Physical adjustments: Generally, you should move away from the oily part of the lane, playing from the inside trajectory with good hard speed, not overhooking the ball.

Players with a fairly straight ball (e.g., Durbin or Schlegel) might wish to play straight up the boards (from approximately the first arrow), never swinging the ball to the right, but keeping it on line to the pocket.

CROSS-WIPE CONDITIONS

Here the oil is distributed heavily in the center and then wiped toward the gutters. This does not affect your shot.

DRY HEADS BACK ENDS

Here the heads can be dry, allowing less than the necessary skid in the first 20 feet. Obviously, this starts your ball out wrong, so the rest cannot be perfect either. As in the spotty lane condition discussed previously, the ball's roll will be uneven, and consequently its accuracy and power will be affected. As it approaches the sparsely oiled back end, it stops and goes into its hook, creating a very difficult situation to deal with.

Type of ball: hard urethane or hard plastic

Physical adjustments: A good way to combat this condition is to loft your ball farther down the lane. If your loft is approximately 1½ feet, for example, then you would increase it to 3 feet to meet the condition.

IDEAL CONDITION

Is there one condition that most bowlers will agree is best? One is the situation in which the heads are heavily oiled to give the ball its skid, with the oil stopping approximately three-quarters of the way down the lane. The back end would be dry, allowing the ball to hook, with the outsides lightly oiled. Here you are able to get your slide, roll, and hook, and, because of the concentration of the oil, the lane will be more apt to stand up to play for a longer time.

The adjustments that this situation allows a bowler to make are many, thereby increasing his chances of scoring well.

Type of ball: moderately soft urethane
Physical adjustments: none

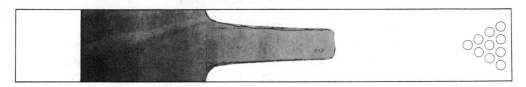

LANE CONDITION REVIEW

Some general rules of thumb apply to lane conditions and what you should expect from them. Use the general guidelines below to improve your game and to help you make the right adjustments when the lane conditions call for them.

BALL ACTION: OILY VS. DRY CONDITION

Oil decreases your hook since the surface allows your ball to slide more readily without biting into the lane surface. Without the bite or friction, the ball can't dig in to hook. Dryness, on the other hand, dramatically increases your ability to hook, as the ball is able to bite into the surface and gain traction. Like a car on ice or snow, equipped with chains or studs, it's able to dig in and turn. When the lane is oily, your ball reacts like a car without chains: your wheels spin feverishly to no end.

Naturally, the more oil, the more skid, so that the relationship of skid, roll, and hook previously outlined becomes distorted. An increased skid in turn affects the roll and hook. Once distorted, you cannot expect the desired result on the back end, as your ball will come up short or too long and miss its mark. On the other hand, if the lane is dry, the skidding is decreased, allowing the roll to come into play and establish the proper balance of the skid-roll-hook relationship.

In the oily situation, the result at the back end will be a reduction in power, since you've not been able to get the roll and hook to snap into the pocket. Therefore, less drive will result, and, instead of driving through the pins, the ball will deflect and not strike. Obviously, the opposite results on the dry surface, where the ball can whip into the pocket, due to the traction causing it to drive through.

SPEED AND LANE CONDITION

Oil will increase your speed because there is less friction between the ball and the lane. Extra speed may seem deceptively beneficial. But the result is that your ball won't roll and hook as it must to snap the ball into the pocket. This is caused by the lane, not your physical game. And it's really a "negative" speed because it causes your ball to bypass the other important factors (roll and hook).

On a dry lane, your friction is greater, reducing the speed of your ball, causing it to skid less and roll more. But rolling reduces the ball's speed further because a greater ball surface area hits the lane surface than in the skid and because of the increased friction due to lack of oil. To make sure it doesn't slow down too much, you will have to throw the ball with more physical speed.

HITTING POWER AND LANE CONDITION

Your ball can enter the pocket either high or light. Since the ball hooks more on a dry lane, the hits will more than likely be high hits on the nose. On an oily lane, the ball hooks less and comes up light. Light hits can create pocket splits, while high hits might create nose splits (see Chapter 3).

These are just general ball reactions to the conditions mentioned. The fun starts with compensations you make for any negative conditions. You'll rarely find an ideal lane condition waiting for you, so you'll have to make the conditions ideal through

At left, a high hit; at right, a light hit.

your own adjustments. Often you'll have to use a combination of adjustments to handle each unique situation.

The table that follows, "Marshall Holman's Guide to Lane Conditions," is a handy reference to use in adjusting for various conditions. But again, before you blame the lanes, run through your physical checklist. Are you making any errors in the basic elements of approach and delivery?

PHYSICAL CHECKLIST

APPROACH

- Speed
- Timing
- Spot
- Walk
- Coordination

DELIVERY

- Release
- Follow-through
- Body position
- Slide
- Balance

If you find problem areas on your checklist, you'll have to use trial and error to determine what type of solution is best. The solutions you should try are discussed more fully in Chapter 4.

MARSHALL HOLMAN'S GUIDE TO LANE CONDITIONS

The table on page 117 is intended to help you identify existing lane conditions. The first part of the guide helps you run down the checklist of your physical game before you blame the lanes to determine if this is your problem. After honestly eliminating each element of your physical game as the source of your problems you can move on to lane conditions as a possible cause of poor shots.

A NOTE ON FAST AND SLOW LANES

Lanes are often referred to as being either fast or slow, which is determined by the ball's hooking ability. The fast lane is one that has a highly oiled surface throughout, and the ball does not hook with great authority. On the slow lane, on the other hand, the ball hooks more readily.

Often these terms are interchanged, causing confusion, since the characteristics discussed deal with two different items—the lane and the ball's ability to hook. So be careful to understand what the term actually means when it is used.

TOTAL ADJUSTMENT FACTOR

To put lane conditions into realistic perspective, let's review the physical adjustments called for in certain situations. This will give you an understanding of the "total adjustment factor," which is the relationship between the adjustment in your physical game and the adjustments made because of lane conditions.

The amount of hook the ball will display can obviously affect its impact on the pins. You can hit in the pocket, on the head pin, or at any other point in between.

For instance, if the lane is slow and the ball hooks dramatically, crossing over the lane, you should make an adjustment to move a few boards inside, increase your speed, and kill the hook. On the fast lane, this procedure is reversed—moving out, increasing the hook, and killing the speed.

This brief review should give you an idea of how alert and analytical you must be to identify what is needed and to react, as I've stressed before, instinctively. You cannot react instinctively

MARSHALL HOLMAN'S GUIDE TO LANE CONDITIONS

	FULL BLOCK	FEATHERED BLOCK	BLOCKED CONDITION*	REVERSE BLOCK	DRY HEADS/ BACK ENDS	IDEAL CONDITION	TRACK CONDITION
INSIDE	oily	oily	oily	dry	oily/dry	oily	mod. oily
OUTSIDE	dry	mod. oily	dry	oily	oily/dry	mod. oily	mod. oily
BACK ENDS	dry	dry	dry	dry	dry	dry	mod. dry
HEADS	oily	oily	oily	dry	dry	oily	oily
BALL TYPE**	SU/MU	SU/MU	SU/MU	HU/HP	SU/MU	SU/MU	SU/MU
PHYSICAL ADJUSTMENTS	none	none	none	hard speed inside	loft ball	none	straight ball path
SCORING CONDITIONS	high	good	high	low	good	good	mod. good

*For right-handed bowler.

**SU = soft urethane, MU = Moderate urethane, HU = Hard urethane, HP = Hard polyester.

unless you are intimately aware of the situations that may possibly appear. Bowling is a game of surprise; you never know what will happen from game to game, and even from frame to frame, as conditions change.

When I'm bowling in a tournament and our squad covers all the lanes several times a day, I make mental and physical notes of how each lane reacted the last time I bowled it—whether it was hooking, fast, slow, blocked, etc.

The results of these efforts are a reminder and guide for my next game on that lane. Without it, as I run from one lane to another, lane 7 could be confused with lane 17 or 27 as the night rolls on.

If I can determine what existed before and what is happening now, I can pretty closely and quickly evaluate the situation that exists without wasting the time necessary to familiarize myself totally again. Most bowlers do this, and to bowl blindly without notes just doesn't make sense. But keep in mind that lanes change from day to day, so you can't rely 100 percent on your notes.

Lane conditions make the game of bowling interesting, confusing, and, yes, sometimes frustrating. But they're a fact of the game, and you must understand them. Don't hesitate to review this chapter several times—and refer to it whenever you're in doubt. Knowing and being able to read the lane conditions you will be bowling on is the key to achieving a competitive game. Don't allow it to serve as an obstacle to obtaining what you're working so hard to achieve.

6
PHYSICAL AND MENTAL CONDITIONING

Bowlers need a creative atmosphere within which to work, and they establish one by developing their physical and mental game. A high degree of mental and physical energy creates a positive force that allows bowlers to accomplish their tasks.

Any bowler who thinks bowling is an easy way to make a living or that it is easy to become competitive without adhering to strict conditioning is only fooling himself. Bowlers who take this approach will soon find out that those rubber legs and tired arms they're wearing can't make it through the evening.

The physical and mental strain the game can exert on you can be combated only by taking a sensible approach to conditioning yourself to the utmost level you can attain. The challenge that awaits demands this level of dedication!

THE IMPORTANCE OF PHYSICAL CONDITIONING

You've often heard the expression "a sound mind in a sound body." This is a truism if there ever was one—for the two most important gifts that you possess are your mind and body.

The abuse that some athletes visit on their bodies is a shocking and glaring example of total disregard and unnecessary destruction of their finest asset. Fortunately, in today's society, fitness has come out of the closet and assumed its proper place in our lives.

It's hard to believe that our society has put so little emphasis on such an important element of our lives for such a long time. But it often takes a craze to get people moving. Whatever caused the change, I'm not going to argue with it, for the awareness of fitness created by this craze is a positive force for everyone. I just hope its popularity is not a fad, but a permanent direction.

When you participate in a sport, you have to know that your body is the most important asset that has been given to you. It's a miraculous gift. It can withstand some pretty stern tests and persevere throughout. Therefore, to neglect it and then fantasize that you're going to go out and do great things with it is foolish, to say the least.

This attitude exists in some sports, and it sometimes shows up in bowling. To the less astute observer, it looks as though bowling requires very little physical development.

Well, let's dispel that myth, for I do not wish you to find out that after a couple of games you're unable to proceed because you're physically exhausted.

Common sense will dictate that anytime you're required to haul two 16-pound bowling balls around all day and night, bowling some 12–16 games a day, you had better be in shape to make the grade.

Let's be honest. You should maintain this conditioning whether you bowl or not. It's the only body you get.

No matter what you do in the name of fitness, stick with it. If you're in shape, maintain it. You can feel its benefits; don't lose them. If you're out of shape, work gradually to get into it and don't lose it; it will only be harder to regain if you do.

Three factors come into play in physical conditioning—nutrition, exercise, and general well-being, especially prevention of injuries.

The bowler must be acutely aware of the importance of each, for bowling depletes your body of valuable nutrients due to its pressures. It can drain the energy from your body, leaving you limp and ineffective in your total game.

NUTRITION

Nutrition is an important factor, especially on the tour, when you don't eat right because of some of the times you must bowl. It is therefore of utmost importance to avoid junk foods, which will slow you down considerably.

On the tour, your time is at a premium. You just have to do the best you can. It's extremely difficult to be on tour and try to eat healthy foods.

I have trouble getting up early in the morning, not a unique phenomenon of American society. Consequently, I don't have breakfast. I don't feel like eating until I've been up for an hour or two, and if I bowl at 9:00 A.M. I'd have to get up at 5:30 or 6:00 A.M. to have anything to eat to give myself time to shower, dress, and be at the lanes at 8:30 for the 9:00 A.M. squad time.

I also need the extra time because I can't just eat and then go bowling. If I did, I'd have too much food in my system, and I'd be better off not eating in the morning than I would be if I ate and had to bowl with my stomach too full.

I could probably force myself to get used to eating in the morning, but, like a lot of other people, my morning meal has to be timed right.

You will find that you have to do your best eating when you're at home, closely monitoring your intake of food to counteract the effects of doing the opposite on the tour.

If you're on B squad, you bowl at 12:15 and again at 7:00, so you get done with your last block at 10:30 or 11:00. Your next block starts at 9:00 the next morning. You're hungry when you finish. So, if you have a tendency to put on weight and you eat at 10:30 or 11:00 at night and go to sleep, following this routine for about a month or two will give you 10 extra pounds you didn't have before. A lot of young guys come out on tour and put on quite a bit of weight.

It's easy to develop a way out through junk food, and the junk foods usually are those that take a long time for your body to assimilate. You don't want to eat foods of little nutritional value and then be caught with indigestion before a game.

It is therefore essential that you follow some pretty basic guidelines in eating.

- Try to eat fresh vegetables whenever possible.
- Bake, don't fry.
- Fresh is better than frozen.
- Avoid alcohol.
- Avoid tobacco.

- Avoid excessive amounts of sugar.
- Avoid animal fats.

Restaurants on the road are also a source of concern, since you must eliminate those that appear to be less than well kept. Although there is no foolproof method, it pays to pay attention to where you eat. I know I got a case of food poisoning at one stop recently and, though it wasn't serious, it was enough to force me to drop from the number 1 position to number 11 at the end of match play and not make the telecast. Two other bowlers similarly afflicted had to drop out totally.

Imagine coming so far and having to drop out for something like that! It sure is frustrating.

VITAMINS

I believe you should supplement your diet, especially when your eating habits are off because of travel and your squad's bowling times. But I don't believe you should overdo it. That serves nobody's interest. Remember, with vitamins it's not quantity that counts but quality (pureness) and the right dosage. The harmful effects of improper vitamin intake should be stressed more and the public educated. It's an area where many abuses exist. Therefore, it is wise to seek the advice of your doctor before embarking on any vitamin supplementation program geared to your needs.

EXERCISE

No matter what you do, you should establish a daily plan of exercise to supplement your nutritional efforts. When you're young you can get away with a lot more inactivity than you can when the years start creeping up on you.

Exercise comes in many forms. For bowlers, I don't recommend much weight training since the stiffness associated with weight training can restrict your movement and hinder your game. I jog and play golf to exercise for bowling.

Bowling requires endurance, especially in your legs, since they have to hold you up throughout a 42- or 56-game format, and walking and running can increase your endurance. Avoid jogging on hard surfaces, as the last part of your anatomy you wish to injure is your knees. Undue stress on your knees will dramatically reduce your effectiveness in bowling, so use caution when doing leg exercises.

In the past, I used to run quite a bit, anywhere from four to eight miles a day. Running proved to be an excellent conditioner. I have since gotten away from it, but hopefully I'll get back to it again because, besides its conditioning effect, I really enjoyed it. Running keeps your legs strong and improves your heart rate. It makes your whole body strong, and I think it's always an advantage to be in good health, even in a game that really doesn't take strenuous effort for each individual shot. It's not like lifting 400 pounds or trying to take a football 40 yards downfield.

The constant repetition in this kind of sport, as you take a 16-pound object and walk anywhere from 13 to 17 feet with it over and over again, may make you fail to notice that you are wearing down a little bit or getting tired.

It can make a big difference if you're in a little better shape than the next guy. It gives you a better opportunity to do well as the tournament progresses.

When I was running, I wanted to continue it on tour, so even though my time schedule was tight, I made time for it. I would get up a little earlier, or I would run in between rounds. It was a great release when I was frustrated to go out and run. After running for a few miles I would forget about the frustrations of bowling.

Be sure you do the proper conditioning for running. Stretch before and after you run and do not overdo it. If you want to run four to eight miles a day eventually, there's plenty of time to lead up to it. Don't try to go out and reach your ultimate goal too early.

WEIGHT TRAINING

I think weight training has its place in bowling, but you have to be careful with weight training. Don't work on certain muscle groups too much.

You don't want to get too much bulk (size), and that's why I worked with Nautilus equipment for a while. That was a pretty good program, because it doesn't really build up the kind of bulky muscle that free weights do or that some other kinds of weight work would. But even in the Nautilus gym I never used the equipment that worked on the latissimus dorsi muscles because, if you build up your lats, your arm has to go out. If your arm goes out, you can't get the swing close to your body.

Here you would be hurting yourself. It would be better not to work out at all than to build up that particular muscle—unless you're the kind of bowler like Nelson Burton, Jr. Nelson has always worked out, from the time he was in high school as a high school wrestler. His body has developed powerfully, and his game has developed around the way his body is built. It would be very difficult for me to bowl with Nelson's lat muscles, but he has no trouble with that; it's the way his game is built.

Fortunately, I feel I've got the ideal size for bowling, which is approximately 5'8", 140–145 pounds. I don't have enough strength to get the ball down the lane over and over again without becoming tired, but I'm small enough that I don't have to worry about swinging the ball around my hips or having any part of my physical being get in my way.

Swimming, bicycle riding, and tennis are also good builders of endurance.

WARM UP BEFORE WORKING OUT

When you do any exercise it's important to warm up before starting. Just some simple calisthenics will suffice.

It's also a good idea to do a little minor stretching before you start bowling. It doesn't take a lot of stretch to get your leg muscles warmed up.

If you try to throw the ball out too hard when it's been a little cold outside and you're stiff, you risk the chance of straining your groin muscles, which is not that uncommon. Remember, do a little stretching out before you start bowling.

Also, don't try to throw your first ball at full speed. Work your way into it; don't try to throw it too hard.

MODERATION

In designing your exercise programs to supplement your bowling activities, remember to use your abilities as a guide. Don't overdo it. Exercise in moderation, no matter what you do, especially for the nonstop forms of exercise like aerobics and jogging.

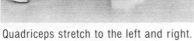

Quadriceps stretch to the left and right.

Toe touching.

Back stretching.

To warm-up before a game, I practice my approach without the ball over and over and over . . .

... and over and over ...

Remember, you're a bowler, not a marathoner. I jog in the early morning when on tour. It relaxes me and gives me a good feeling as the circulation flows.

So devise a sensible program that meets your physical needs without restricting your bowling needs. Common sense is the guide.

PRACTICE

You've no doubt heard the expresion "practice makes perfect," and this is what you're trying to do—duplicate that perfect shot over and over again in bowling.

Practice takes patience—and a great deal of it. Practice can become boring or hypnotic if you don't have the proper attitude toward it.

You will be throwing a ball over and over at the same target. This type of constant duplication of effort can be quite trying on your nerves, especially when you're not executing well. It is then up to you to take the initiative to assess what you're doing right and what you're doing wrong.

You must develop your weaker skills. It's not going to be good for your ego, but it will help your game. To practice your strengths instead of your weaknesses will only make the latter get worse. This will mean that all the adjustments you make will become limited due to the limitations of your physical skills.

Practice must be conducted in the proper atmosphere. Push yourself and create a challenge each time you practice.

Your ultimate goal in practice is to establish an intimate relationship with your skills through total concentration when you execute them.

If you fail to bowl seriously or establish what you're doing wrong, you might as well fold up the tent because you're heading down the road to frustration and ultimate failure. But most bowlers faced with this sad result will still lament, "But I practiced. How did this happen to me?"

Environmental Adjustments

People are a product of their environment when developing their styles in practice, and I think this is probably true in many sports. If a golfer learned how to play on a course where you have to play the ball from left to right, he would learn how to fade it or how to hook it, and the same thing is true in bowling.

An important part of physical conditioning is being a well-rounded bowler. If you grow up near a bowling center where you can throw the ball fairly straight and get away with it, or if you have to throw the ball straight, you're going to. If you grow up in an environment where you need more power on the ball, you're quite lucky. This is so (especially today) with all the great power players we have on tour. Mark Roth was the first, in the '70s. I was fortunate enough to come out on tour at this time.

It was almost as though Mark and I were bowling by ourselves for a few years. We were the only ones who could take advantage of the power game. Now, with all the power players on tour, a lot of the kids watching on television see the way the pros do it and try to copy them.

Still, when you get to a certain point in the game of bowling, you have to do what works well in your own area, and that's all you can do. You can't continue to try to hook the ball in a bowling center where the guys throwing the ball straight are doing the best bowling. You're eventually going to start throwing the ball straight.

The same is true for people who throw the ball straight in a condition where hooking the ball is better. You have to learn how to hook the ball a little bit more.

When you come out on tour you're supposed to be able to do everything. And you need to do everything to a certain extent. I'm never going to throw the ball as straight as Ernie Schlegel or Mike Durbin, and there are some guys on tour who would never hook the ball as much as I do or Mark Roth used to do, years ago.

Mark Roth is a good example to study. When he first came out on tour, he hooked the ball more than anyone, and now he throws the ball fairly straight because he's learned through the years of being on tour that power playing is good, but power plus accuracy is better. This is one of the reasons why even today Mark is consistently great.

You should always try to do what's natural. I like to hook the ball, but there are certain conditions under which I could throw it straighter. It's difficult for me to throw the ball straight from the right of the pocket. Now, if I get to where I'm right in line with the pocket or inside, around the third or fourth arrow, I can throw the ball straighter, like I had to in the 1985 U.S. Open.

When you're throwing the ball straight from the third or fourth arrow, it's as though you're hooking the ball. You're to the left of the headpin when you're delivering the ball, even when you're throwing it straight. You have to throw it a little bit to the right to get it to the pocket!

Now, if I'm playing the second arrow and I'm throwing the ball straight, I'm throwing it "up the boards," or actually at a left trajectory to the pocket, which is extremely difficult for me to do.

I like to take the ball and throw it to the right and bring it back. If I'm inside a little deeper, I can actually use the same method but keep the ball on line a lot straighter.

So, in practice, keep an open and thinking mind to adjust and be flexible where needed.

GENERAL WELL-BEING: INJURIES AND OTHER PROBLEMS

BALL FEEL

One of my major concerns is to have a consistent feel of the ball in my hand. You want the ball to feel like an extension of your body. If you can get that feel, you can eliminate so many things you have to think about in your physical game. All you want to think about when you're making a shot is hitting your mark and following through, making the best shot possible.

If my ball feels like it's going to fall off my hand in my backswing, then I feel I'm forced to squeeze it. If I squeeze it, I won't get the loose roll on the ball, and the result will be taps if I hit the pocket or even worse if I don't.

Any departure from your natural style can lead to injuries, and it's important that you avoid these setbacks.

I always have on hand tape, cork patch, etc., which I use in the front of the holes to take up some of the excess. When I drill a ball, I always drill the thumb hole small and work out the sides where my calluses are.

I put a "shure-hook" or a cork patch in the front of the hole, and I put tape underneath the cork patch. Then I can take a little tape out or put a little tape in and make any minute adjustments that will make the ball more comfortable.

I also do something that people always ask me about: "Gosh Marshall, I watched you bowl. It looks like you're kissing the ball. What are you doing?" "Are you kissing the ball for luck?" What I'm doing is actually blowing a little air into the thumb hole. This is like putting in half a piece of tape; it takes up a little of the slack. The warm air makes the inside feel a little tacky. I also use a resin bag called Sta-dry. I pound that into the finger and thumb holes and then wipe all that stuff off. A little residue is left in the holes to give me a better grip.

I take all these precautions to ensure a proper feel and to eliminate or reduce the incidence of injury due to an improper feel of the ball.

I often feel as though I'm losing the ball on the backswing, so I need that secure feeling when the ball is in my hand. I can pull my game in other places to compensate.

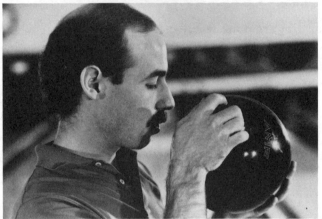

Am I kissing the ball for luck? No, just blowing a little air into the thumb hole.

But with the sweetness of the grip can come the bitterness of increased friction, which can cause injury to the hand. To prevent this, I use a lot of patching with collodion and cotton or nylon patches to keep the friction off my thumb.

INJURIES

The most common injury in the last few years has been tendinitis. What I do to prevent this is to get an elastic bandage and wrap it around my wrist just to try to tighten things up a bit. It doesn't tighten things up to the point where I lose freedom of motion, but it keeps my wrist a little more secure.

Wrapping Your Hand

A lot of friction is involved in releasing a bowling ball. As a result, many bowlers cut their hands and blister under calluses. Even when their hands become sore they have to continue bowling.

Patching has become a blessing for many players, including me. I use the cut patch material even before my hand is sore, as a precautionary measure. If I didn't, it would take only two or three games for my thumb to become very sore. So I put the patch all over three or four spots on my thumb where I generally get sore, and that helps out a lot.

Broken Finger

Broken fingers don't occur often in bowling, but when they do it's very easy to control the injury and the healing process just by waiting until the finger heals. However, sometimes such an injury may occur when it's inconvenient to take time off from bowling.

I broke the fifth metacarpal in my right hand, which is the second knuckle of the little finger, in Akron in 1982 at the Firestone Tournament of Champions. I was upset, and I was bowling on the end pair (39/40). I left a 10 pin and got so mad that I hit the wall with my hand. So one good way not to break your hand is not to hit walls.

That year was a very strange one for me. I had to miss a few tournaments because of my broken hand.

In Syracuse, the very same year, I had just finished a qualifier, qualifying third for the telecast, and Terry and I were going back to our room at the Howard Johnson. We also had our dog with us. Terry walked through some sliding glass doors, with the dog following her. I was following the dog. The dog started back out the door, and Terry closed the door to keep him in. The dog didn't get out, but neither did my hand. I broke the same finger again.

I was scheduled to bowl on the televised finals the next day, so I didn't know what to do. I was really upset and didn't want to miss the finals, so I went to the emergency room that night and they confirmed my belief that the finger was broken. I explained my circumstances to the doctor and asked him about something I had read about—the use of Xylocaine or Novocain in sports to deaden pain. I didn't know it for a fact, but I had heard they use it in football so that players with injuries can go out and play. I asked the doctor about it, and he said there was no way he would give me that because I could do so much damage to myself by using it. He said that in my situation it would be too dangerous; he wouldn't prescribe it and didn't know anybody else who would.

So all he gave me were some chemical ice packs; you break the ice pack, and the two solutions mix and get cold. He said, "Freeze it and try it. Your body is only going to let you do so much, and if you keep it numbed up a lot you may be able to bowl."

So, after not getting any sleep that night, being up most of the night at the hospital, I got up the next day and called a friend of mine who has a pro shop in Syracuse. I had Cliff Celebra drill out a ball for me that was two or three sizes bigger in the thumb and both fingers. Instead of a 16-pound ball, I used a 14-pound ball.

All I wanted to do was see if I could just bowl, and if I shot 170 or 180 and didn't totally embarrass myself, I would feel that was all right.

I won my first match against Mal Acosta, shooting 258.

In the next game I bowled against Dave Soutar. I shot a 236, and he shot 260. I lost that game, but it could have been one of the best stories in sports if I had won the tournament.

Fortunately, I had been playing a fairly deep inside angle, but because of my broken hand I opted for the outside line. Since I was throwing a lighter ball, I felt the outside line would give me a better line to the pocket, with the lighter ball helping my chances of striking. It worked very well.

Fortunately, the hand has healed, and no stiffness, pain, or lack of motion is evident.

MENTAL CONDITIONING

As discussed in the preceding section, physical conditioning, in its total sense, is an important aspect of your competitive game. The importance of this factor in all sports has been emphasized continually, but until recently its obvious partner shared less than center stage and quite honestly was overlooked by many.

In the past, too many athletes were oblivious to the mental conditioning aspect of sports. The ability of a select few to survive under pressure while others faded or crumbled proved to make the difference between winning and losing. But this ability was attributed to certain "superhuman" talents, making the hero bigger than life and often placing him on a lofty perch that portrayed his abilities unrealistically. It has now become obvious to us that the difference actually should be attributed to these athletes' mental game and conditioning.

In today's hectic society, it is a wonder that anyone can condition himself mentally. Planes are delayed for hours, traffic jams exist everywhere, and monumental obstacles are placed in everyone's path. Mental conditioning is the ingredient that often brings success, not only on the athletic field but also in every other endeavor of life. So we better take a close look at mental conditioning; its benefits may have some far-reaching consequences beyond the lanes.

The triangle formed by physical skills, physical conditioning, and mental conditioning serves the very important function of allowing us a means of assessing our mental game as with the other elements. I call these levels of distinction.

LEVELS OF DISTINCTION

Each bowler has the ability to develop to a certain degree each particular aspect of the triangle. Often, various factors affect the development of one area over another. For instance, in the physical game, natural skill, practice, adjustments, etc., come into play. Physical conditioning includes commitment, development, etc.

Some bowlers are just better fighters than others, and they strive for higher levels even if their actual physical game doesn't really afford them the opportunity to reach those levels. I think you can make up for a lot of what you lack in your physical game by just how badly you want it mentally. If you really want it mentally, I think you can do amazing things. There were many bowlers who bowled with Earl Anthony on the tour who were Earl's equals as far as physical talents are concerned. I didn't say they were better, but they were equals. But mentally, nobody touched Earl Anthony. In fact, nobody was even close. When Earl got going, he was able to sustain the drive to bowl one good game after another. He did it not just because he had such a great physical game, but also because he was so much stronger mentally than anyone else. That's what put him so far above anybody else who has bowled since.

Not only did Earl think he was the best, but I'm sure that most of the other bowlers and the fans felt the same way. All that positive energy going for him, coupled with his physical game, held his level of distinction above that of all others.

Awareness of the mental game recently surfaced at the 1984 Olympics in Los Angeles. Sports psychologists were employed to strengthen the American athletes so that they would be mentally prepared to compete in the games. This event signaled a message to a nation that sports is more than just a physical contest.

It's no wonder that, in a sport such as bowling, which pits one athlete against another before a crowd of people, the mental ramifications are many. For some top professionals bowling in the televised finals, whose skills are evenly matched, the mental game can make the difference between a win and a loss. For once the match starts, your mind becomes the controlling factor and it can communicate to you early on whether you're going to win or lose. The area we are exploring is often critical to your success, especially if you want your game to improve to the competitive level.

BOWLING PERSONALITY VS. STREET PERSONALITY

These two factors can be very different indeed. In fact, my own personality is often misunderstood because of my reactions to bowling situations. I am placed in a quandary, having to decide whether to depart from my competitive game by not reacting naturally or to do what works best and achieve results.

I can remember when things weren't going too well for me. I would get tons of mail from fans saying: "You gotta get mean, Marshall." "You're losing the fire!" "Let go!" It was as though they missed the explosive Marshall on the lanes and figured that I was departing from my natural game and losing effectiveness. I can't say that they were wrong either, because I'm most effective when I act natural, and that means reacting to situations as they happen. I don't anticipate them, but simply react to what occurs. By doing this, I have most assuredly developed a bowling personality different from my everyday personality. I think with me there's more of a change than others. If I were to be the highly intense emotional person off the lanes that I am on, I think I would go crazy.

Outside of my workplace I like to think I am a calm and sociable person. If I were to react to my dog digging a hole in my backyard the way I react to a 10 pin in a crucial match, I don't even think the dog would like me, and he likes everybody.

I'm much more at ease when I'm not bowling or at my work. I'm very pleased that that's the way I am. I would hate to be so much on edge when I'm at home. I only wish some of my detractors could have dinner with me to see that side of me.

It's really hilarious to see some people criticize my demeanor on the lanes. I'm not hurting anyone with my actions but, as some people feel, adding color and pizzazz to the game through my spontaneous animation. It is often the same critics who fail to recognize that each and every one of us assumes a different personality when we go to work. It's sometimes our defense mechanism that helps us succeed in the workplace. If you're a boss, you probably act overpowering to maintain your position, although this may be totally the reverse in your family life. It is important to note that personality changes only to achieve the desired results. When you become competitive in bowling you've made a decision to take a step beyond mere enjoyment, so your personality may change too.

When I bowl, my personality is serious. I'm dedicated to a job and to doing my very best every time I approach those pins. Nothing else matters at that point. The pins are my challenge, and I use every ounce of energy to focus on them.

I don't think people understand that that personality is necessary for me to do well in my job because there aren't that many people on the tour who undergo such a change in their personalities when bowling. I don't think the bowling fans feel that it's necessary. But some die-hard Holman fans know it is, as evidenced by the mail I get.

I've got all that talent off to the side to draw from, but it takes a pretty big monkey wrench to tap into it.

The comparison one viewer made was that I was like a Ferrari in a Volkswagen dealership because of my demeanor, and this comparison points to the tendency I have to stand out because I'm more emotional than most of the players. It's just the way I work. We all have to do what's necessary to bring out the most in our game, and that's all we can really hope for.

If you get the most out of yourself, no matter what you're doing—bowling, working in a factory, or whatever—that's all you could ever want from that part of your life. Therefore, it should come as no shock that I react when I've put in so much effort and the result is less than I wanted. This desired result is, on each and every first ball, a strike! Approaching it any other way would be a mistake, although I realize I cannot throw a strike every time. I must let my bowling personality think differently in order to maintain my level of distinction.

In my profession, I'm paid for performance, so I'm rewarded monetarily for doing better. But, even if you're working in a factory (as I once did) and you get X amount of dollars an hour, you can still fell better about yourself (as I did) when you come home knowing that you did a good day's work. You may not be rewarded anymore from a money standpoint, but I think that almost all of you would feel better if you felt you'd accomplished something to the best of your ability. It's a degree of professional satisfaction you obtain that's enjoyable.

It is no different with you when you bowl; you must develop your bowling personality from the minute you start to bowl. Learn how you feel about the sport and yourself. Use both to develop a positive bowling personality. Don't attempt to emulate a past or present professional, thinking this will make you successful. All you're doing is postponing the development of your own personality or destroying your game by being someone else. You're you, and that's important, because no one else can be. Don't try to change, because this reality is essential in building both your regular and bowling personalities. Don't be afraid to develop your bowling personality, for once you lace up a pair of shoes and pick up the ball, a new person may surface. Realize this and use it, not worrying about what others will think. Feel free to express yourself on the lanes. It's natural and a necessity in developing your bowling personality, because it's what will make you a better bowler and add to your level of distinction.

One caution to observe is that, just as the worker needs to leave his work personality at the workplace, so do you.

We all know the dangers of bringing the job home, and a sport is no different, especially if you're bowling to achieve professionalism or to play in competitive leagues.

You can't spend hours talking about what went wrong or what might have been. You must leave your bowling personality at the lanes and assume a different role, as I do.

You can do what's effective on the lanes with your personality, but it may not be as desirable off them. Make the distinction wisely, for it will help you deal with a lot to come.

ATTITUDE

As in the development of your personality, your attitude plays an integral role in your success on the lanes.

To develop the proper attitude, you must have a positive outlook. In bowling, it means you must enjoy what you're doing and be willing to make the necessary changes in your life to find a place for it that suits your needs. By establishing this relationship, you will develop an attitude that is, more often than not, positive about the sport.

An integral part of this positive outlook is confidence, and it doesn't matter what professional sport or what job you're in. Everything is so competitive that you have to make a believer out of yourself before you can succeed.

You may say, "I know, Marshall. I want to bowl. I've felt it for a long time, and I do have a positive outlook!" This may be so, but all too often your decision may be predicated on the wrong facts or your decision made for the wrong reasons. Unknowingly, these reasons or facts will play subconsciously on you and change your attitude into a negative one.

When I first came out on tour, I was really nervous, competing against the best bowlers. After a few weeks, as I was looking around at the top stars I had watched and idolized for such a long time on Saturday television, I realized for the first time that they had all started in approximately the same position as I had, with a dream of doing well, not knowing whether they could or not.

But obviously they all started somewhere, and that was at the bottom like everybody else, no matter what the field of endeavor. If you believe in yourself, while forcing yourself to think you're good, you can achieve great things because you're developing the proper attitude. That is what I tried to do—almost kid myself into think that I was better than I actually was.

I really didn't know how good I was when I first came out on tour because I hadn't tested myself under the circumstances, and nobody knows how well he can do on the national tour until he actually gets out there. You just have to be there and test yourself against the best under those types of conditions—traveling around the country—until you know whether you can make it or not. You can't go out thinking you have no chance, for that's the quickest road back home.

If you feel you've got no chance against these types of players, that's exactly what's going to happen to you; you'll end up failing. You'll go home and say, "I could have done very well, but I didn't"—the old "life of regrets" theory.

If you go out feeling like you have a chance, then you have much greater possibilities of doing well.

You have to be able to block out negative thoughts that may surface, for they will change your positive attitude. If you are always on guard in this manner, you will be able to approach things with a positive attitude to achieve the things you want to. No one succeeds with a negative attitude; sooner or later it will catch up to you.

It is here that you must distinguish among your attitudes toward your game, yourself, your fellow players, and fans. The game can represent a hurdle that is sometimes insurmountable, so that action has a positive effect in releasing negative forces. If you hold them in and don't react, your attitude will change; but by releasing some form of reaction you can move on, forget what happened, and so maintain your positive outlook.

Don't get angry at yourself; you don't need an adversary within you. If you take it out on your fellow players or the fans, you will be making a mistake, for it can ruin your total image and not be in line with that positive attitude you seek.

If you address your bowling game in a positive manner, the chances of achieving the results you desire are greatly increased.

Confidence

You must develop confidence in yourself to be a successful bowler. As mentioned before, if you feel you can't do it, you won't. You can only accomplish things consistently through confidence in yourself and your abilities.

This comes partly from being honest with yourself about the true level of ability (distinction) you possess. It's meaningless for someone to foster hopes of a professional career with no chance of attaining it. This is not confidence, but foolishness.

Be confident in your abilities and their ability to improve. Your reward will be confidence in yourself that will improve your game. Your confidence will help you create a positive environment that allows concentration, attitude, and more to flourish and add to your mental game.

Appearance

Bowlers read their opponents and detect when somebody's feeling down about his game and the way he's working. You notice it in the pace of a bowler's delivery or the way he walks. I think that when you see someone like that you have a tendency to bring yourself up even higher, because you know you've got a wounded bird at your mercy. You have to take advantage of everything you can on tour.

If you find yourself in this emotional state, you would do well to throw back your shoulders and walk proudly back to your chair, not letting your opponent know you're fully done in. This could help bring you out of your depressed state and rejuvenate your positive attitude.

PREPARATION

Just as you leave the job on the lanes, don't let your home follow you to work either. You've made the determination to become a competitive bowler and you have to think bowling and nothing else while you're on the lanes. Your start at home or the hotel room and the trip to the lanes can prove to be a very good place to begin your preparations.

You know what you're going to do that evening or day, so when the time arrives, start to get yourself mentally set. Relax by tuning out all other thoughts so that your mind is free. When you feel comfortable, allow thoughts of the match to come into your mind. Don't force them to come; just let your mind think what it wants. If negative thoughts come in, be prepared to counteract their effect with positive ones.

Lay out your equipment, get it ready, and pack it. Don't rush. Make sure you have plenty of time to get to the lanes; leave a cushion for last-minute adjustments to equipment and other personal needs. The main element to avoid is rushing, which creates confusion. After rushing, there's no way you're going to settle down. Use your positive attitude to surround yourself with an air of professionalism as you assume your bowling personality.

This is true whether you're bowling professionally or after work with friends. The pressures initially may be manifested differently, but in our competitive society the participants feel them strongly, even if they only want to prove they can do well in front of the office personnel.

In any event, it's important to feel good when you are going out to compete. Sound basic? It is, but it's still ignored often! If you let your nerves get the best of you, you will soon find that your preparation will become more and more difficult and even impossible. The impending game should be viewed as a pleasant event, not as a grueling battle. That will happen soon enough later on; don't wear yourself out beforehand.

Relax and prepare yourself to assume a positive frame of mind. When I am preparing to go to bowl, there's much more uncertainty at the start of the tournament than toward the middle or the end. At the start, I am basically hoping that I pick out the right aspect of the game for practice the day before. Then I can go out and just make the right shots and learn which I'm making errors on early in the tournament.

As amateurs, it's important that you go with the idea that you will try to do well, but if it's a league and not a big tournament situation, I think it's important to realize that you're going to have a good time.

If you're working an eight-to-five type of job and go to bowl a seven or nine o'clock league, or whatever, it might be best to approach the game as an emotional and mental release. You've been working all day and shouldn't be taking it quite as seriously as I would take it. After all, it's my livelihood.

I remember when I first started bowling in adult leagues back in Medford. I would be just as pumped up in those adult leagues as I am now for the tour or even more so. But I did have fun and enjoyed it. Now that I bowl for a living and have been in the game for 11 years, there's not all that much fun involved in bowling on tour for me. It's mostly work, and that's the way I take it.

I don't go to the lanes to have a good time; I go there to work. If you're bowling in a league, you should go to have a good time and to do the best you can. If you have an off night, it should not be that crucial to whatever else you might be doing; it's just not that important. Even though in leagues there's a little money involved, it's still not like going to work, where making a big mistake can really cost you your job.

CONCENTRATION

If you don't have the ability to concentrate, forget about bowling competitively. It's the essential ingredient that makes the difference in making the changes you need to win.

Concentrate on the game at hand. If you played your opponent last week and did poorly, forget it. This is a new week and a new game. Each frame is to be addressed separately, not with thoughts like "If I get a strike here and a spare next . . ." Think solely about *this* frame and make *this* ball the object of your concentration each time to get a strike.

If everybody were equal physically (fortunately for me, they're not), I would say that concentration is 65 percent to 75 percent of the game. You need a good physical foundation, but unless you have the capacity to think your way through a tournament or league, you're going to have a lot of problems. This is especially true on the tour, where there's so much talent. It's the people who can get themselves into the right frame of mind to bowl and keep themselves there through many emotional peaks and valleys who do well. On tour, you get a three- or four-bagger, and you start feeling good. Then you throw the ball a little slower and get a wide-open split. Now, all of a sudden, you're down in the dumps. You have to be able to ride out those storms and continue to think and work, because you never know when that big game might be coming to bail you out, putting you in a position to win a tournament when you thought you weren't going to cash in at all.

So, to psych yourself up is a positive form of concentration. I look at the people who are ahead of me in the standings, evaluating their game and my game, which usually makes me feel like I have more talents or a better game than they do. By doing this, I'm psyching myself in a proper way to work harder at my game.

I usually do this after I'm done with six games and I'm not in the lead or in the top 24. I'm looking at the board, saying, "If he bowled so well that block, and if he did etc., etc., I know I can bowl better than he can for the most part." This makes me bowl better.

I think a lot of top bowlers do this, for the look up at the board can be a blueprint to your game plan, as you compare the other bowlers' deliveries, etc., to yours.

Now, if I look at the board and find 24 guys who throw the ball totally differently from the way I do, then I might say that this week is not going to be too good a week for me. But that very seldom happens. While I do depart here from concentrating on my opponent's game, it never happens when I'm playing him.

Concentrate on your game, not on the other guy's. I can recall a game in Akron, when I was bowling in the Tournament of Champions, following Mark Roth's pair. I went over to see Mark bowl and saw that he was playing about three boards deeper on the lane than I was and was doing well. So I adjusted my game to his and lost the match! I should have been concentrating on my game and not his. Since I missed the cut by 11 pins, it might have made a big difference if I had concentrated instead of allowing myself to be distracted. You can't be influenced by what is happening with other players. It's got to be done all on your own. It's too easy to watch the other players and think that you can get a really good reading from what they're doing.

Often, by watching your opponent, you can break your concentration. Bowling is a game in which luck is a factor, and often a lucky break that results in an opponent's strike will have you wondering if you allow it to. Forget his game and concentrate on yours, because your game is the only thing that will beat him. Don't concentrate on your opponent, but on yourself.

Distractions must be blocked out; they destroy concentration. Your mind must be free to allow only thoughts affecting the shot presently confronting you to enter your mind. As a distracting thought enters, you must block it out and avoid being pulled away from your game by another game close by. You can't do anything about the game three alleys away, so don't let the cheers of the crowd affect your concentration. Keep your mind on your lane.

If a totally intolerable situation occurs (e.g., a solid hit and an impossible spare), don't go off the wall. If your bowling personality can't take it, your concentration will be shot.

If your first ball fails to strike, shift your mental gears to think spare, funneling all your concentration to achieve it. You have no alternative, so you might as well concentrate on what you have before you. By doing this, you will be able to address each situation with a positive attitude and proper concentration.

Breaking Concentration

I'm the only one who can break my concentration or keep it. I feel it's up to me. The only problem I usually have on tour occasionally, which occurs more in match play than in the qualifiers, is that some of the slower bowlers have a tendency to break my concentration. After a few games of match play, it seems as though one side of the house is bowling a little faster than the other, so if I have to watch for 10 or 15 minutes in between games, it's hard to keep my concentration together.

This is a very difficult situation; it seems the faster players are always at the mercy of the slower players, who are dictating the pace of the tournament. Since the slower players are not going to speed up to the pace of the faster players, the latter have to wait until their slower brethren are done with their game.

The fans are very close to the bowlers on the tour, much closer than they would ever be in a professional football or baseball game. Since they're that close, they have a tendency to want to talk to you or ask for your autograph while you're in the middle of your games. This happens even though at the lead-in to every block the tournament director always says, "PBA regulations prohibit the use of flash cameras and the signing of autographs during competition. The bowlers appreciate your cooperation," etc. Many people forget about that or have gotten there too late to hear the announcement. Since you're so close and, being faster, you are done and are just sitting there, they feel it doesn't do any harm to come down to ask you for your autograph.

This is a difficult situation for the bowler because this person is coming up and asking you for your autograph, which is really a compliment. However, they don't realize that it's a very inopportune time. You have to tell them that you're sorry, but it's against regulations and that they should see you when you get done. You know, sometimes if you're having a tough round, it's hard to do that in a really nice manner. You have to choose your words wisely when you're talking to the fans.

HANDLING PRESSURE—STRESS

You've developed a positive attitude and concentration that should prepare you mentally, but the pressures of bowling create varying situations that require adjustment. Sometimes these adjustments can prove to affect these two facets of your mental game.

Pressure, in some instances, serves as the catalyst that makes you perform to a higher degree, but at the point at which pressure no longer serves as a motivator it is dangerous.

Bowling again is different in that you cannot release this pressure by running or skating about, following the flow of the play, but you must sit and wait for your turn. It is during this period that pressure can mount and become destructive. At this point, you must concentrate on *your* game and thinking of ways to improve it, etc. You must visualize your next ball, working it out in your mind and going through the video in your mind, blocking out all that is happening.

Maintain your positive attitude and let it work for you. If your opponent strikes, so can you, and if you do your best, you will win.

Don't think ahead; it pays no dividends. You're going to try to do your best each frame, anyway. Thinking too far in advnace, you will forget about the present.

Now try to relax! Yes, just relax. The tension is building, the pressures are on, you're at the stress point. Go limp for a few seconds. Let your tensed body relax and concentrate on something positive. Although you may have left the lanes for a few seconds, you may have left tension and stress there for your return.

Take a deep breath as the pressure builds. Now release it. To your amazement, the pressure will subside.

Everybody handles pressure in different ways. If you're fortunate enough to be able to bowl on tour and make a living, then you must have something going for you. All you can do is just throw one ball at a time and make it the best shot you can possibly make. It doesn't do you any good to get nervous; it only adds more pressure and defeats the objective you're out to accomplish.

There are other ways to try to calm your nerves and release pressure, putting yourself at ease in a pressure situation.

For instance, I would say everybody on tour spot-bowls. When I say "spot-bowl," I mean looking at either the dots or the arrows that are 10–20 feet down the lane or picking out a board to look at that might be a little darker that you will be trying to hit. A good way to assure yourself of making a good shot in a pressure situation is to exaggerate your focus on that particular board. When you actually throw your ball, continue to look at your mark until the ball has gone well past the mark. That will make you reach out better for a more fluid shot.

If you're bowling in match play, you may not want to watch your opposition. There are quite a few bowlers who do that, due to the fact that there are a good many lucky shots involved in bowling. If you happen to be watching your opposition and he gets a real lucky shot, that can have a tendency to make you get uptight or feel a little unlucky.

So, if you don't watch your opponent (as we said before in concentrating on your game), you don't have to worry about what he does. If he gets a lucky strike, you don't even know about it. Likewise, if he's playing a certain line on the lane and you watch him, you may think that line will work for you. Everybody's ball rolls differently, and just because one particular bowler is playing the second arrow, it doesn't mean the second arrow is going to work for you.

So, once again, don't be faked out by what the opposition is doing. Concentrate on relieving pressure, on what has gotten you to that point of the tournament, and on what you can do to stay there, move ahead, and win it.

Learn to relax and control your thoughts, and you will be able to cope with pressure. If not, you will become a limp bundle of nerves that will not be able to bowl, let alone become competitive.

PACING YOURSELF

One important way to cope with pressure is to be sure to pace yourself so you don't expend too much energy at any one point.

A good example of the need for pacing yourself happened to me back in 1981 in Miami, during a televised match. I led the tournament and was challenged by a bowler named Bo Bowden from Texas. Some people in the crowd were getting on my case a little bit. I think I started out with a spare and got four strikes in a row. I was really animated and intense, being pumped up about the title match. In the sixth frame I left a wide-open split, and a group of people in the crowd got really excited because it made the game closer and they were rooting for Bo—or maybe they were rooting against me. Whatever they were doing, it really got to me, and it was a very uncommon split—the 3-4-6-7. I shot the split and made it! When I made it, I guess I unleashed possibly every bit of emotion that was in me.

Unleashing all that emotion left me drained for the last four frames, and I lost the match! That outburst cost me the match by leaving me no energy to concentrate on the last four frames.

It was a very rough lesson to learn. At the time it cost me $11,000, a title, and the momentum I had gained on tour. I was then having my best winter tour ever. It was the 10th week of the tour, and I had already won three tournaments. I had an excellent opportunity to win my fourth, which would have put me over $100,000 in just 10 weeks. This would be an exceptional start, to say the least.

I got so emotionally involved with that one split shot that I just lost my competitive edge. It's that easy.

So you shouldn't expend too much energy at one time. I find that when I'm in a tournament I try to pace myself a little bit by starting off in the qualifying not trying to have too many highs and lows, but just trying to be even-tempered. As the qualifying stretches on into the later stages of qualification, I become a little more emotional. As the match play runs down to the last few games, I'll become more emotional, letting things flow a little bit more and, during the television show, usually letting it all out.

Even in the match play or the television matches I try to exercise some self-control. As I said, with Bo, I lost my competitive edge because I became a little bit too excited that time. If I had made that split and gone through only half as much emotional outpouring as I did, I probably would still have had something left to continue the match.

TEMPER

Basically, you want to keep yourself fairly even-tempered, but it depends on what kind of player you are. If you're an emotionally active player like I am, you have to watch it a little more than a player who just throws the ball and sits down without showing a lot of outward emotion.

But repressed emotions can get to you if you have a tendency to get upset, even if you don't show it. You may need to let off steam a little bit at a time. You don't want to let things build up and build up until there's finally a major explosion.

A couple of bowlers who used to be on tour would never get upset over any one incident, but they just let things build and build until finally they became so upset with themselves that they couldn't do anything. Maybe if they had shown a little emotion outwardly and let it seep out a little bit at a time, they would not have been faced with that great big buildup and frustration and would have been able to continue bowling better.

This is not an unknown phenomenon in sports, but it surely is one that's misunderstood. The souring of an athlete is often due to the inability to release frustration or emotions. It would be a good thing for teams, leagues, etc., to identify this syndrome before it gets advanced, because some of the problems in sports today (drugs, violence, etc.) are associated often with a souring due to this emotional problem. Early detection in any sport is, and should be, a primary function of governing bodies and an obligation to their players, who test themselves under the toughest conditions. It would save a lot of black eyes for some sports and, more important, the future of a human being.

AWAITING YOUR TURN

While you're sitting there waiting for your next turn, what should be going through your mind? If you're bowling well and doing things properly, you should try to key in on what things are going right. If you're doing something wrong, don't just sit there and think of nothing while you're waiting. Try to think of ways to accomplish your goal—to strike on every ball.

You know it's not a realistic goal, you know you're not going to strike on every delivery, but you do want to give yourself the best possible chance to make the best possible shot each and every time.

When you're having a little trouble, you might consider going to a different ball or speed or maybe throwing it straight or hooking it more. But these are just a few possibilities; use all of your knowledge of lane conditions and the physical game to make the necessary adjustments.

DEVELOPING MENTAL AWARENESS

To be a successful bowler, you must be a thinking bowler—always aware of what's going on, but using this knowledge to your benefit.

Be aware of negative forces that affect your game. These may translate into many things, such as the wait in between turns or the bowlers next to you or fans behind you. By developing an awareness of these negative aspects affecting your game, you can use this ability to neutralize their negative effects.

Instead of overreacting to the wait between turns, becoming nervous, anticipating or even imagining what your opponent will do, you must turn this negative aspect into a positive force. Use the time constructively to adjust your thinking, prepare your ball, adjust your glove, or whatever will help to keep your mind off it.

It may pay to use the "stop thinking" technique. When the negative aspect approaches you, substitute pleasant preplanned thoughts to counteract it.

Your awareness of negative influences on your game can be dealt with by using them as points of encouragement or motivation. Overcome the trauma of their negative nature and use them as a signal to relax automatically, using your concentration while taking deep breaths to get past the moment. This awareness can translate into positive identification measures to seize opportunities.

Knowing your optimal level of energy will allow you to use more power in your ball release when you need it or to relax when you're reaching your saturation point.

Awareness of what your body needs at various times in a game plays an integral part in developing a consistent mental practice technique that allows you to be totally aware throughout the game, frame by frame, making assessments, evaluations, and the adjustments necessary to meet any situation.

You should set your sights on becoming a thinking bowler, capable of adjusting mentally as the game unfolds, balanced in your approach and adjustments, but continually aware (mentally) of all that is happening.

The ability to use the awareness of both positive and negative forces in your game to your advantage can be the determining factor as your opponent struggles to meet his challenges.

BOWLERS BECOME FANS

It's very easy to sit in your chair and become an observer. Don't get too comfortable watching your opponent. If a game gets further out of reach, you may have a tendency to watch your opponent, instead of concentrating on your own game. When this happens, all is lost, and you might as well congratulate your opponent.

You've basically given up all the characteristics we've discussed before and left your game.

This happens to everyone when they first come out on tour; it certainly happened to me. I spent more time in my first tournament watching the other players than I did concentrating on what I was doing, because I had never seen these players in person before, so I thought it was pretty neat. There I was, saying, "There's Dick Weber over there and Don Johnson, Dave Davis, and Carmine Salvino, and I'm bowling with Harry Smith. Gosh, this is fun! How come I'm averaging 180?"

This happens to about 95 percent of the people who join the tour. There are, however, exceptions. One of them is Mike Mcgrath, who won the first tournament he ever bowled in. That was phenomenal. There are also few bowlers who have done well in their first few tournaments because most bowlers feel they're a lost cause since they are not focusing on what they are supposed to be doing.

Likewise, don't act for the fans or care what they think. It's not important. If you try to please them instead of concentrating on bowling your game, you've made a big mistake.

Don't become awed by your opponent. Rather, use this as a positive force to help you do better.

ESTABLISHING THE OFFENSIVE STRATEGY

Can a sport like bowling have this type of strategy? By all means! When you're feeling good and do everything right in practice, you can feel it. So, instead of coming out relaxed, you come out like gangbusters and use your positive energies.

This may blow your opponent out of his chair, but realize that you can't get a strike every time. So don't get so high that you can't come down or expend so much energy that you can't finish the game.

Offensive strategy is your own ability to make good shots; you're not allowed to trip your opponent.

It's like playing pool. When your opponent is up there, you're not allowed to say anything or do anything; all you can do is hope that your opponent doesn't bowl better than you.

There are certain times when you feel you have to go for the strike. Going back to the Tournament of Champions, I was having trouble on one lane in a particular game. I was coming in light on it. I was coming in high on it; every time I came in high I'd make an adjustment and come in light. Finally, it came to the 10th frame, where I needed to strike to pull the game out and save it.

There was no reason to try to shoot safe, so I had to try to jam the ball into the pocket. That was a very offensive move. I moved back to where I was coming in high, and I just tried to throw the ball a little bit harder and straighter, to force the ball into the pocket. It worked in that particular instance.

Determine what is needed to establish an offensive edge and use it wisely.

DEFENSIVE STRATEGY

Defensive strategy does exist, but it has a very limited role in bowling.

If you sit back lethargically, the game will pass you by. But if a spare such as the 6-7-10 comes up, you may play the 6-7 to get the count instead of going for the spare, especially when you're in the lead.

If you're bowling in a match play situation, especially on television, and you have the match well in hand, then you might want to think more of just keeping the speed up and making sure the ball doesn't break through the nose. You're not thinking so much about getting the strikes as about staying out of trouble. On the other hand, you don't want to play it too cautiously, because if you do, you may find yourself faced with open frames in another way.

I remember Earl Anthony was doing a Q & A a couple of years ago and somebody asked, "What do you do differently on the 12th ball when you have 11 in a row for a 300 game?" He said, "You don't do anything different. If you got the first, you try to do exactly the same thing you did the first through 11th times."

If something is working well and things are happening the way you want them to, stay with that particular shot. Try to use the same speed, the same roll, the same line, etc.

Don't fall prey to being too cautious. You can find yourself behind with no way to get back again.

MENTAL INTIMIDATION

Yes, intimidation is used in bowling, but not physically. Instead, there is reputation intimidation, where a bowler will be intimidated by your record or name. It causes some to fall apart and others to try harder, since you're the big name to knock off. So it goes both ways.

Verbal intimidation has no place in bowling, but some bowlers will pass remarks to break your concentration or irk you. It's best to ignore these comments since the reason behind them is only negative and your return comment can do nothing but serve as a source of encouragement.

Many players are intimidated when they come out on tour, and they're made to feel like they should be more on guard than is really necessary. They don't feel like they can be as loose, as vocal, or as animated as they might normally be.

The intimidation they sense is a combination of things but is not anything the veterans do intentionally. I feel it's the respect the rookies have for the veteran players plus the organization itself, the PBA, which can be a little forbidding. For example, Harry Golden (our tournament director), if not my closest friend, then one of my closest friends on the tour today, is an imposing figure. When I first came out on tour, he appeared to me as an authority figure, and he can be very scary to a youngster coming out on tour for the first time. After all, he's been there on the road for 20 years, and he has a very serious look about him while he's working. His professional air can create an atmosphere that some young-sters term frightening. Once you get to know him, he's really just as easy as anybody. He does his job with as much knowledge as there is, and nobody could do it any better. He's got a hard job, and he's a pretty fair man and a nice guy.

I know that, because I've had a very good record in bowling, the other bowlers often work harder, which makes it more difficult for me. They might get a little lax in playing against other bowlers and they may be in 23rd place in the top 24, with a few games to go, and then come up against me. They say to themselves, "I'd sure like to beat him. I'm going to work a little harder to beat him!" Sometimes it works to their advantage and to my disadvantage. Now, instead of an easy match I have a tiger by the tail.

I've done the same thing, where I've been low in the top 24 with a few games to go, and I'm bowling against somebody who's up near the top. It makes me work a little bit harder.

One incident concerning intimidation comes to mind, and it happened in Edison, New Jersey, in my sixth or seventh tournament. I was confronted by a couple of bowlers, only one of whom I remember. It's kind of funny, looking back on it, because at the time he was hardly a veteran player himself, but he had been out for a year or so, and he was accepted by the rest of the tour and sort of palled around with a lot of veteran players.

So Joey Beradi came up to me and basically said, "Marshall, if you don't watch the way you act while you're bowling you're going to have a tough time on tour." This is not verbatim, but he said something like that. Joey and I didn't get along well for a few years, but I just had dinner with Joey at the last Milwaukee tournament, and we were laughing about that occurrence, which happened some ten years ago.

GETTING STARTED

Positive Influences

The toughest thing on tour is to get started—to win the first tournament or to make that first big finish—because until you have that first big finish there's nothing to fall back on mentally. You could go back to what you did in a league one night or in some local tournament, but it's not the same as being out on tour. You have to work extremely hard to get that first positive experience so you'll have something to draw from.

I know when I first came out on tour it didn't really help to think about the time I won the tournament in Tacoma or Eugene. Those seemed very insignificant, even though it's the same process of throwing a ball. Only the names are changed.

But you really have to have that initial positive experience on tour, I think, to draw on to give you positive energy. It doesn't happen all the time, but sometimes you have a sense of oneness with the ball, the lane, and your body, and you feel you can do no wrong. At other times there's a lot of apprehension in the way you think before you make a delivery. It is here that negative influences can take over your game.

Negative Influences

Even if things are going badly, you can look inside and say, "I know I'm the best bowler on these lanes!" Will this make the difference? Not necessarily, because certain situations sometimes arise in bowling because of lane maintenance and conditioning. In these cases, no matter what kind of talent you have or how strong you are physically, it's hard to overcome what the lane maintenance people have done to the lanes. There are also a variety of different ways of approaching the delivery. You can move farther in or farther out, throw harder or slower, hook or change balls. You've got so many alternatives, it's like a golfer going out with a hundred different clubs. What he does is to take any one of those clubs and choke down or step on it a little bit, or he can hit it high or punch it low or whatever he feels will help.

You can make many adjustments to counteract negative influence, but it's up to you to find the proper adjustment. So with the different lane maintanance conditions you encounter from week to week, sometimes you just never find the right combination.

If I could know in advance the proper way of releasing the ball, it would be an edge. Imagine if somebody could tell me, "You need this ball with this weight distribution, this speed, this roll," etc. I could think, "Well, that's where I'll play." But you have to figure that out for yourself. The game is only 10 frames long, so there are occasions when you never figure out how to combat negative influences on the lanes.

There's no way, for example, to go out to the lane and run your finger over the lane surface itself to determine where the oil is in heavy concentrations or light coats. Even with this knowledge, you don't have all the answers, because oil is not the only condition that controls the game; lane surface also does. If the lane surface is really worn, it might take twice as much oil. You could use just a little bit of oil and get the same result as if you poured gallons of oil out there.

So that's where the people who are doing our lanes—Lon Marshall, Jim Tebucci, and Bobby—really have to make as many educated guesses as the bowlers. They do the best they can, and they have a totally thankless job. Each week, they have only 1 satisfied customer out of 300. So combat the negative influence intelligently.

ASSESSING YOUR MENTAL GAME

Getting back to the bowler's triangle, you need to assess your mental game. The following checklist will provide you with some general elements that constitute a good mental game. You must be honest in answering these questions to derive the benefit this exercise will give.

1. Have you developed a bowling personality?
2. Do you maintain the proper attitude?
3. Do you prepare before your game?
4. Do you leave yourself enough time?
5. Are you able to concentrate fully?
6. Can you handle pressure/stress?
7. Have you developed awareness?
8. Do you have confidence in your abilities?
9. Do you prevent intimidation from affecting you?
10. Do you know your level of distinction?

For every "yes" answer, give yourself 10 points. Add the total number of "yes" answers (e.g., $4 \times 10 = 40$) to obtain an assessment of the overall effectiveness of your mental game (e.g., 40 percent). The percentage obtained should indicate the level you've reached.

The mental conditioning required to reach your established goal of becoming a competitive bowler is immense. If you don't apply yourself, you will soon learn that physical skills are not enough, even when coupled with physical conditioning. You may assume some level of competitiveness, but nowhere near that which you can have by mastering all three aspects.

Work hard to achieve what you want in life, both on and off the lanes. You have been given natural gifts; use them wisely and within the levels of your ability.

Whether you're aspiring to be a professional or just a good bowler in house leagues, play the sport for your physical and mental pleasure.

7
THE PROFESSIONAL BOWLER
—THE TOUR

The culmination of your efforts could lead to the Spectacle, as most people call the telecast, one day each weekend afternoon. The ability to make it on the tour and display your talents before a nationwide television audience is a misunderstood phenomenon. The effort, skill, determination, and perseverance that are needed to succeed on tour are transparent qualities that escape the eyes of the viewers who enjoy this wonderful sport.

Let's take a look at what happens if you are fortunate enough to make the tour.

It's a long way up to the status of professional bowler and the tour, but the distance that separates a lofty dream from reality is not insurmountable. If it were, I suspect that bowling's ranks would have a very slim roll call.

The ability to do anything in life is founded on most of the principles we've discussed here, for bowling is a profession just like law, medicine, etc.

The job description might read:

WANTED: PROFESSIONAL BOWLER
Athlete with top physical skills, willing to travel extensively and make substantial capital investment in his future—must

be self-sustaining individual, able to meet the high standards of a national organization, and handle the extreme pressure of a high-powered situation. Salary will be according to your performance. Interested parties please contact . . .

The ad speaks for itself; bowling on the tour is a test of your abilities and a challenge. It's hard. I would not underestimate that fact, but it's not impossible. Let's take a look at making it on the tour.

MAKING IT

The requirements to become a professional bowler are not quite as stringent as perhaps they should be. A few new rules that came out of the last executive board meeting state that you can't get your card and come right out on the national tour, as was previously the case. The rule change became effective January 1, 1984, and requires new Professional Bowling Association members to establish their level of competitive ability. This is gauged by the new member's ability to cash in two of the association's regional tournaments.

By meeting this requirement, the new member will be allowed to bowl in national events that are held in his region only. The PBA regions are shown below.

Professional Bowlers Association Regional Breakdown

If the new member is looking toward competing on the national tour during his first year, he must cash in four regional tournaments.

Once these tour privileges are attained, the bowler is subject to an annual performance review. There are minimum standards that must be met in order to maintain the privileges. These are, for the following year to cash in at least one tournament or to maintain a 190 average in PBA competition in the prior calendar year.

New members must also meet the application requirements for new membership in addition to completing a required course at the PBA member's school within one year of their application. This school is mandatory and a prerequisite to retaining membership in the PBA. The course is designed to introduce new members to the PBA and to explain what is required of them.

Some of the subjects covered by the course are as follows:

- Developing Human Resources
- Professionalism
- The PBA: Its History, Accomplishments, and Goals
- Finances
- Lane Maintenance
- Alcohol and Drug Abuse Information
- Bowling on Tour—Rules
- Dealing with the Media (PBA Staff)
- Exam Evaluation

Member's School I is a three-day seminar, covering the above subjects.

APPLICATION

As with joining any organization, you must fill out an application. The application for membership in the PBA appears on pages 159–160.

The application requirements are also listed in order to meet the association's standards before application.

So this is the paperwork that gets you in the door.

I feel the new requirements are a good thing—a way of protecting the youngsters who want to try to make a living on tour. It's

MEMBERSHIP APPLICATION
PROFESSIONAL BOWLERS ASSOCIATION

I am interested in (check one) NATIONAL MEMBERSHIP ( )   REGIONAL MEMBERSHIP ( )

FULL NAME (print) ....
                        (last)   (first)   (middle)

HOME ADDRESS ....

CITY .... STATE .... ZIP CODE ....

HOME PHONE ....(.....)......................... BUSINESS PHONE ....(.....).....................................

DATE OF BIRTH & WHERE .... SOCIAL SECURITY NUMBER ....

HOW DO YOU WANT YOUR NAME TO READ ON YOUR SHIRT ....
                                                                    (print)

SHIRT SIZE (check one) Small ( )   Med. ( )   Med.-Large ( )   Large ( )   Extra Large ( )

HOW DO YOU WANT YOUR NAME TO APPEAR ON MEMBERSHIP CARD ....
                                                                    (print)

In the spaces provided below, have the Regional Director or any Regional Representative in your region sign his name. If this is not convenient, obtain the signatures of three PBA members in good standing.

1. ....
      (signature)   (PBA #)   (address)   (city, state, zip)   (date)

2. ....

3. ....

LIST ANY ASSOCIATION, GROUP OR COMMITTEE, OF WHICH YOU ARE A MEMBER, WHICH IS DIRECTLY OR INDIRECTLY INVOLVED IN, OR WITH, BOWLING ....
....

Your best three all-time tournament performances (name of event . . . where it was held . . . year it was held . . . high game(s) . . . high series).

....
....
....

READ BEFORE SIGNING

This application must be accompanied by a recent black and white photograph of the applicant, three (3) letters of character reference from prominent people in the community (other than relatives), the form completed by the local American Bowling Congress association Secretary, and a check or money order in the amount of seventy-five dollars ($75), which will be kept in escrow until accepted. If application is rejected, your initiation fee will be returned. Allow approximately six weeks for processing and applicants will be notified of acceptance or rejection immediately. Upon receipt of application, all applicants subject themselves to the Constitution, By-Laws and Tournament Rules and Regulations of the PBA and are entitled to the rights and privileges of an Apprentice Professional.

I understand that coverage under the PBA group insurance program for members accepted after their fortieth (40) birthday reduces by one-half when they become sixty-five (65) years of age.

SIGNED... DATE...................................

Regional Directors and Representatives are listed on the letter covering this application.

Courtesy of the PBA.   ©1983 Professional Bowlers Association of America (PBA)

VERIFICATION OF APPLICANT'S AVERAGE
TO BE COMPLETED BY YOUR LOCAL AMERICAN BOWLING CONGRESS SECRETARY

Please provide **complete** information on applicant for the two (2) most recent seasons, **based on a minimum of 66 games per league.**

NAME OF APPLICANT (please print) ....

APPLICANT'S AMERICAN BOWLING CONGRESS NUMBER ....

SEASON NO. 1 (most recent) 19____ (year). List all leagues (attach note if more than four).

Name of Bowling Center and League	Average	Total Pinfall	Total Games
1.			
2.			
3.			
4.			

SEASON NO. 2 19____ (year). List all leagues (attach note if more than four).

Name of Bowling Center and League	Average	Total Pinfall	Total Games
1.			
2.			
3.			
4.			

NAME OF LOCAL ABC ASSOCIATION SECRETARY ....
(print)

WHERE HE MAY BE REACHED ....(..........)...................
(address, city, state, zip code)   (phone number)

REMARKS ....

....

....

I HEREBY VERIFY THAT, TO THE BEST OF MY KNOWLEDGE, THE ABOVE-LISTED IS TRUE.

SIGNED ....   DATE ....
(Local ABC Association Secretary)

built-in experience that they have to have before they come out and actually try the national tour.

One requirement that has been an issue of controversy is the requirement to have a 190 average for the last two years in 66 games or more prior to making application. Some people think the average should be higher, but this would cause problems.

In some areas of the country, the requirement is probably appropriate; in others, it might seem too easy to meet. It might actually lead some youngsters to believe that they might have a chance to make it on the pro tour. But the fact of the matter is that bowling lanes can be made easy and they can also be made difficult. A 190 average in one bowling center might be the equivalent of a 215 average in another center, just depending on the lane maintenance. This is true, for instance, when the house uses the process known as *blocking the lanes*, where they put a heavy concentration of oil in the center of the lane and a light concentration or no oil on the outside part of the lanes. When you throw the ball out, it hits the dry part and hooks back. You pull the ball, it hits the oil, and it holds up, so instead of having maybe an inch to hit 15 feet down the lane to strike, you might have 8 inches. It's amazing how you can take a lane and make it easy or difficult.

Raising the average requirement to 200 wouldn't be fair to the people who bowl in difficult centers. It would make it almost impossible for them ever to reach the requirements to make the tour. Basically, the requirements are not that strict; a 190 average over a two-year period is probably fair.

You also need the endorsement of three members of the PBA (in good standing) or the endorsement of the regional director or regional representative.

Those are just a few of the things that are necessary to try the tour. Also, the school requirement must now be met before you can go out on the national tour. You can still bowl on the regional level, but the national will be on hold until completion of the course.

APPRENTICESHIP

When I first came out on tour, I was an apprentice, and as an apprentice you're the lowest man on the totem pole. The way I got into tournaments was by filling out the entry cards I received for the tournament dates and sending them in. If you're an apprentice, the postmarked date becomes the date on your entry card.

That's how they line up who is going to make it into the tournament. If you get your cards in too late, then you just get shut out of tournaments. If there are that many people entering (and there always were when I sent those cards in), it is a little nerve-racking waiting to see if you've gotten in.

I was shut out of two tournaments when I first came out on tour, and that was before they had what they called the "pro qualifying" or the "rabbit squad." The way they have it set up now, that doesn't happen anymore because they have prequalifying to get into the tournament much as they had in golf a few years back, although golf has gone to an all-exempt field.

What happens with exemption is that exempt players have that day off, and there might be 200 or more prequalifiers trying to qualify for maybe 30–50 spots. They take the high scores, and they are entered into the tournament. It's very difficult, not just from the standpoint of how many make it out of a large number of people who are trying, but also because there are not that many games and there's really no time for mistakes in the qualifying round of the tournament. You have from 18–24 games of qualifying in a rabbit tournament. A prequalifying has 10 games, and in these games, if you have a disastrous game, the other 9 games are sometimes not enough to come back. There's a lot of pressure on those rabbit bowlers to make the grade.

So, getting that card is only the start, for, obviously, you have to do your work beforehand. When (and if) that first block is out of the way, you must face the reality of how you are going to sustain yourself financially out there—our next subject for discussion.

BOWLING'S ECONOMICS

You are faced with basically two methods of financing your new challenge: through a financial backer or using your own funds (or your family's).

If you're fortunate enough to have your family be able to sponsor you without too much trouble, that's probably the best way you could have it.

Unfortunately, very few guys who come out on tour have the luxury of having enough money themselves or in their family to enable them to make the tour. I feel it's too difficult to come out on tour with just $5,000 or even $10,000 and try it for 10 or 15 tournaments.

THE SPONSOR

I feel you have to have somebody behind you who will trust you and believe in you and give you the opportunity to spend a year or a year and a half to find out if you have what it takes to make it. Even if you have all the talent in the world when you first come out on tour, there are very few people who come out and suddenly start doing really well. That happens very seldom, so you need to have the money behind you to keep you out. You don't want to have to start thinking, "Boy, I'm not doing very well. I better start eating at restaurants that don't cost that much," or "This motel is not so nice, but it's $5 less, so I'll stay here anyway."

You have enough to worry about, just trying to compete against the greatest bowlers in the world. You don't need the extra hassles, so money is not just very important; it's extremely important.

Most bowlers are sponsored by local businessmen who are usually avid bowling fans and bowl in a few leagues a week themselves. This is one way for them to get involved with a pro sport, because they feel as though they have a stake in the pro bowler's tour. So for a businessman who has the money that he can afford to gamble with, and it certainly is a gamble, it's also an enjoyable way to help somebody start out in a professional sports career.

One pro bowler cannot back another bowler, but your sponsor doesn't have to register with the PBA. It would create a conflict of interest, for instance, if I were sponsoring just any bowler and he made the top 24. If my bowler was up near the lead and I was having all sorts of problems in 22nd place, I could just let him win if we bowled each other, and it wouldn't be fair to the other bowlers. In the past, there were players who helped other players along, but that's now subject to a very strict and heavy fine.

THE FINANCIAL ARRANGEMENTS

The arrangements with the backer depend on each individual, whether the bowler approaches the backer or the backer approaches the bowler. In my case, I've had two backers, both of whom came to me. I wasn't really looking to go out on tour, but it just happened.

A gentleman in the lumber business back in Medford, whom I knew from bowling in leagues, was a league bowler with probably a 160–170 average. He really enjoyed bowling and wanted to put me out on tour. Unfortunately, he didn't have quite the financial assets that he led me to believe he had, and I ended up bouncing checks.

When you're 19 years old and in New Jersey, and the tournament director comes up to you and says, "Marshall, we got a check for so much money, and it didn't go through the bank, and you're responsible," it's very difficult. I don't know whether it was that he had had the money at the start or that he never had it, or that he had business troubles. No matter what the reason was, this is one of the dangers too many youngsters could face when they come out on tour. Some youngsters will take anything (backing) they can get, and you really have to make sure that the relationships of the sponsor and the bowler is one of great trust.

The sponsor has to be able to trust you with his money; on the other hand, you have to be able to trust the sponsor. When you're 3,000 miles away from home, and your checking account is down to $100, you must be confident that he's going to put a few thousand dollars in the bank so you can do what you need to do and what you have to do on tour. The sponsor has to have faith that you're going to use that money wisely; the relationship is based totally on mutual trust.

You must not let your desire to get out on tour blind you to what stands before you. Sometimes there is no way to tell about a potential sponsor, believe me, and it is a most frustrating situation when everything looks really good and then goes sour. The effects of this type of experience could prove a major hurdle for some to get over.

So I ran into a little trouble with my first sponsor, who wasn't putting the money in that I needed to continue on tour. It was a matter of luck that when the tournament director told me about the problem with the checks that I happened to be doing well in a particular tournament, so I was able to take the money I made on the tournament and pay the PBA for the checks that had bounced and continue to stay out on tour and have enough money to go home.

It was really lucky the way it worked out. I finished third in that tournament in Edison, New Jersey, in 1974, and I made $2,400. I don't remember exactly how much I had to pay back the PBA, but I paid them, and I thought I had enough money for the last seven tournaments of the year. However, in the first six of the last seven I didn't make a dime, so I went through every cent I had and had just enough money to get home.

I was out on tour for 13 weeks, 7 with a sponsor, and I cashed in on four of those tournaments, two of which were top-five finishes. Not making a dime the six tournaments that I was on my own for was mentally difficult for me to accept at that particular age. The money I had left amounted to a couple of thousand dollars! I knew that was it, and I truly feel that affected my performance. I was very fortunate, though, that I secured another sponsor just before the start of the 1975 winter tour, and that came about in a very interesting way.

I wasn't looking for a sponsor. I had sent in my reservation cards for the tour, and I don't know why because I didn't have any money. I was just hoping that something would happen as I was sending them. I didn't know what I was hoping for, but I was still hoping that it would happen. I was really fortunate, since I had written a letter to the PBA a day or two before I received a phone call from a friend of mine about a gentleman in Seattle. Mike Kelly was the friend, a good one. Mike also bowled on tour. He told me there was a businessman in Seattle who was very interested in sponsoring me, and he gave me his number. I then called Jim Roberts of Seattle. After our telephone conversation, I flew up the next day, and we got everything settled that day.

So I wrote a letter back to the PBA, telling them to disregard my last letter, which cancelled me out of the tournaments I had initially entered.

The deal wasn't the greatest in the world; Jim gave me eight weeks. He said, "We'll see what happens in eight weeks." For those eight weeks the pressure was on, and in that period of time I was lucky that I finished in the top 24 five times; in the other three tournaments, I cashed. So, out of eight tournaments, I made money eight times. Needless to say, my sponsor and I were both very pleased, and that relationship lasted from the winter of 1975 to about the 1979 season.

Jim and I stayed together for quite a long time. My percentage kept getting better, and he was very satisfied because I was doing well. You could never meet anybody who was more of a bowling nut than my sponsor, Jim Roberts. He's a pretty good bowler who, depending on lane conditions, can average 180–200. Jim would bowl in four to six leagues a week. He was an absolute bowling fanatic; he loved the sport, and I know he had a lot of good times with me, serving as my sponsor.

He came out to the Tournament of Champions in 1976, and he saw me win the tournament. In a way, this was like his winning the tournament, because he was a part of what I was doing. I know that was quite a thrill for him, and I won many other tournaments while we were together. We had a really nice relationship. I don't see Jim very often today, since he moved from Seattle to the San Juan Islands off the coast of Washington.

Jim took me from a position of just being at home and having no chance to a position of opportunity. He's very much responsible for my doing what I did in those years and what I've been doing in the last three or four years since I've been out on my own. He really helped me out a lot, so to Jim I say, "Thank you! You're a true friend and fan of the sport."

STRUCTURING THE BOWLER/SPONSOR RELATIONSHIP

As in most situations of backing, the arrangements that are made assume a clandestine aspect that prohibits disclosure to those who seek guideleines when entering a sport.

This type of restriction on new participants only makes their job unnecessarily harder, for I feel it's the obligation of former novices to share their knowledge and experiences with their younger counterparts. They ought not to sit back and say, "Well, he's got to learn the hard way." Obviously, this attitude helps no one, and instead of generating respect between the younger player and the veteran, it perpetuates an unnatural feeling that only selfishness or self-interest creates.

In the end, an open line of communication between the young-ster starting out and the veteran can benefit the veteran, since the younger participant can infuse new ideas, thoughts, and, yes, even financial incentives that have a domino effect that benefits every-one on the ladder.

It is this sharing of information and ideas that represents an obvious solution to some sports ills. Disclosure works for, and not against, everyone to promote the sport and the people who put on the show.

So with this in mind, let's take a look at what the arrangement should and could be. Governed like any other business deal, its success depends on the intentions of the parties and their flexibility to understand each other's needs, commitments, and sense of fair play. It is when contracts are interpreted to the letter of the law that problems start with harsh feelings, actions, and accusations. Make sure this does not happen. Openly discuss any problems and share the joy of positive performances. It will create a balance that can only benefit the relationship you need with your sponsor.

For the most part, the bowler and sponsors start out with about a 50–50 split, *after expenses.*

This is the norm when you first start out on tour, but most of the kids who are trying to go out on tour can't be too picky about their sponsorship deals. It is here that you must be cautious, but also prudent enought to assess what's being offered and what you expect, for if the offer is much lower than your expectations and you take it with half-hearted interest, it can only serve as a negative force later on in your relationship. Therefore, your approach and acceptance must be founded on many bases to substantiate the relationship. For instance, although you must consider that you want more or feel you should get more, you may have to lower your sights because no one is going to offer you a better deal. So you may have to decide between going out and just forgetting it. This decision is not usually a hard one.

So younger bowlers are generally willing to give more to the sponsor than they might have to, but they're so pleased that they could find somebody who would be willing to put them out that they take almost anything.

ANALYZING DEALS

To aid you in making your decision, you must analyze your position before entering into a relationship so that the mathematics don't become a shocking reality later on. This is really pretty simple, but it is somehow overlooked in these anxious moments.

To look at this factor, set forth the following projection sheet, which determines what you expect (income) and what you feel you might be able to make out on tour. Remember, this is solely up to you, and you must be hungry to attain it, while being realistic in setting the figure. You cannot become complacent with those dollars your backer is putting up. He's not adopting you, but merely providing the necessary funds to pay your *expenses* in order to make income. It is here that some people have a problem rationalizing what the deal is, so get it straight from the beginning. You're the money-making man here, not your backer.

CONTRACTS

I recommend that you have a written contract no matter who's sponsoring you, unless it's your family.

As lawyers say, contracts are subject to various interpretations. Imagine how complicated things would become if you had to depend on someone's memory or understanding of a verbal agreement. Don't rely on a verbal contract; it can be a nightmare. I think it's important to have something in writing that binds both you and your sponsor to perform specific actions.

As I found out in my first relationship with a sponsor, you sometimes need an extra little push to make sure your sponsor complies with the contract terms. I did have a contract with that first sponsor, but he breached the contract when he failed to put money into my checking account.

INCENTIVE PROVISIONS

Any new player coming out on tour should have a contract that provides incentives. One such incentive would be a provison that, if you make × amount of dollars, the split is 50–50, but if you make a little bit more, the percentage changes in your favor. For example, if you made $30,000 or $40,000, the split could be 50–50, but it would go up to 55 percent or 60 percent if you made $50,000, and if you made $70,000, it would again rise accordingly. I don't think this represents overstepping the negotiating boundaries or that this would be objectionable to a backer since these types of incentives will obviously benefit both of you.

These possible adjustments can reflect a significant change in your projection sheet to serve as an added encouragement to do better.

Approach these contracts realistically; a contract is only as good as the people who sign it. If the intention of one or both parties is to ignore or violate its terms, it's not going to be honored no matter what it says. It boils down to trust and commitment.

Again, even if you have a contract, and it's breached, it's not going to help you out on the tour. Your remedies are limited, often to courts of law whose calendars are clogged and can in no way meet your immediate needs.

So approach the situation intelligently, letting your feelings guide you. If a negative thing happens, look at it as a lesson and not as defeat.

HOW MUCH DOES IT COST?

I don't keep track of expenses now as closely as someone who is first coming out on tour. I've been fortunate in that I've done well enough over the years that I don't regiment myself quite as closely as a new guy on tour might.

One week I may spend $600 and the next $900.

I think a new guy coming out on tour could make it on only $500 to $600 a week if he drives. If he's going to be flying, it's naturally going to cost more—probably an extra $100–200 a week more.

When you're coming out and you're by yourself, I think flying is a better way to go. I drive the tour now, but I've got Terry with me and our dog, Cutty, so it wouldn't be easy to fly the tour with Terry and the dog. But when you first come out on tour you're usually coming out by yourself, and you don't know that many people, so driving across the country all by yourself would be quite an awesome task.

No matter what the cost, don't gamble with too little money just to try out the tour. Your efforts will invariably be drained by financial worry, which will affect your performance on the lanes.

The bottom line on the tour is trying to make a living, and it's a very difficult way to make a living. It takes a lot of dedication. The expenditures that bowlers have to pay for by themselves always must be taken into consideration.

Bowling differs from being part of a baseball team, where you get your salary of X amount of dollars during the year and the team picks up the plane fare, hotels, food, and all the incidentals. These expenses have to be made by the bowler, so you're looking at making the first $20,000–$30,000 in a year to take care of tour expenses and the next $10,000–$20,000 dollars to take care of expenses at home. The money that you make after that is actually money you get to keep after it is split with Uncle Sam. So, it's a tough way to make a living. It's getting better, though. More players now have an opportunity to make money on the tour than there were when I first came out. It seems when I first came out that only the top 20 players could really make a living. Now, it's true of about the top 40. Even with the cost of living being significantly higher in 1985 than in 1974, there are more bowlers making a living today than there were 11 years ago, and I think that's a significant change for the better in bowling.

We continue to get the good ratings with our Saturday afternoon telecast, which is very positive. The network is very happy, and we're very happy to be with ABC during the winter time and in the spring. NBC started doing our fall telecast in 1984, and the USA network is picking up our summer telecast, so all our tours are televised. We're getting good exposure, and I feel we desperately need the television. Without television, we wouldn't have the corporate sponsorships, and they go hand in hand. If this weren't available, it would be a big pot game, with the bowlers playing for their own money. This would make it very difficult to stay on the tour.

So address your financial dealings intelligently and use the guidelines I've given you as a rule of thumb. Be flexible and assess all the pertinent considerations. Don't rush things; take your time.

ON THE TOUR

Once you've tied down those contractual and financial considerations, you are ready to step out into the world of the tour, and one thing you'll have to get used to is traveling.

I don't really like the travel, but I look at it as a trade-off, for I like what professional bowling has done for me and traveling is part of what it means to be a pro bowler. If there were some way that I could mail or phone in my scores, I would do that, but you have to be there, and that means traveling from Miami to Hartford, from Seattle to Los Angeles, and to all points in between.

When you get out there, the tour is like any other job. You've got to get used to the schedule and be up for your performance. So the tour has its timing, and you need to adjust to it.

IMAGE AND RESPONSIBILITY ON TOUR

The PBA sets strict standards for its participants and includes those guidelines as a part of its school training. Likewise, a publication that accompanies every application spells out those guidelines even further. Write to the PBA for a copy.

I once asked Harry Golden, our tournament director, this question: "It just seems like I'm being scrutinized a little bit closer than the other bowlers. If I do something and get in trouble, and if somebody else does the same thing, maybe they don't get in trouble. Why?" He explained to me that, because I'm fortunate to be one of the top players, people were coming in and focusing their attention more closely on me than on others, especially bowlers who don't enjoy the notoriety that I have in the past years.

I think that, because I'm being watched more closely and a lot of kids are coming to watch me bowl, it's important that I keep myself in line. If I do show emotions, I should show them in the proper way.

It's sometimes difficult to do that, but it's important. It's like going to a car dealership and seeing a Ferrari and a Volkswagen. You're going to take a look at the Ferrari because it just stands out more. In fact, an article written some years ago said that I was like a Ferrari in a Volkswagen dealership. That just referred to my demeanor—the way that I have a tendency to stand out because I'm more noticeable than most of the other players. It isn't because I try to be; it just happens to be the way that I work. Everybody has to do what's necessary to bring out the best in his game.

That's all you can really hope for. If you can get the most out of yourself, no matter what you're doing, that's all you can ask. Even in my profession, I'm paid on the basis of performance, so I'm rewarded monetarily for doing better. But even if you're working in a factory and you're getting X amount of dollars an hour, I think you'll still feel better if you're doing your best. I know I feel better about myself when I come home knowing I did a good day's work. I would probably feel better inside even if I were not rewarded anymore from a dollar standpoint.

INTANGIBLE QUALITIES OF PROFESSIONALISM

Everyone has a certain number of qualities that are not visible to most observers. They are the innermost secrets that make them what they are. These invisible qualities of professionalism exist in varying degrees in each person, no matter what he does.

I formerly had a tendency not to pull out as much from my

physical abilities as I should, and that has probably been the single biggest drawback in my professional career.

I see players who, for one reason or another, aren't fortunate enough to have the same physical abilities that I have. But through sheer determination they still do well on tour. It is certainly not a credit to me that I have, at times, not worked as hard as I possibly could and taken advantage of my abilities. I think I'm much better today than I was four or five years ago.

Fortunately, I have enough ability that I can occasionally not work as hard as I should and still do all right. There are some bowlers who have marginal ability, and if they have that tendency not to work as hard as they should, then they're not going to make anything. I know a few bowlers who are like that, and they're not currently bowling on tour.

YOUR OBLIGATION TO THE PUBLIC

I think everyone in bowling must understand that it's the bowling public that enables us to make a living to begin with. So we owe them something. I know there are times when you might have a frustrating tournament or a bad night, and you come out of the locker room to find some kids who want your autograph. You feel like just getting away from the bowling center and getting back to your room in the hotel to be by yourself, but you can't do that. You have to give of your time, because they are the ones— those kids and their parents—who are making it possible for you to make a living. So you have to give them your time and sign the autographs, while answering questions that you probably have answered a hundred times before.

You must acknowledge your responsibility to the fans and the press because it's through the press that bowling has gained the level of success we've enjoyed. Much of our popularity is due to the type of press coverage we've been able to get. If the press didn't want to write anything about bowling, we certainly would not be very successful.

So there certainly is a great deal of responsibility that goes with bowling, and you just can't run away and hide if you have a bad (or even a good) performance. Make yourself available to the fans, the press, the sponsors, and to anybody who wants part of your time because everyone I just mentioned is responsible for the pro bowlers' tour.

BOWLING'S GLAMOUR—THE REALITY

What you see on television is not all that exists, especially in bowling. It's unfortunate that the telecast is all people see of our tour. If you have the opportunity to go to a pro bowlers' tournament and watch the whole tournament, from the prequalifiers through the telecast, you would see a lot more than you'd ever imagine. I know a lot of people expect to see certain bowlers on television, and it's almost as if they think we're automatically seeded in.

In the late '70s and early '80s, Earl Anthony, Mark Roth, and I were making a lot of telecasts, and I think that the fans automatically equated Saturday afternoon with Earl, Mark, and Marshall, not realizing what went into making the top five. It's a long way from the opening game of a tournament to Saturday afternoon.

In our tournaments, we have approximately 200 prequalifiers and then 160 people in the tournament itself, so you are looking at maybe 100 exempt players and 200 nonexempt players going for five spots and eventually trying for the top spot of winning a tournament. Three hundred people a week try to win a tournament! It's extremely difficult.

I had a fairly successful 1984 winter season, and yet I only made it to the top five twice, and my best finish was fourth, which by my standards wasn't anything to get overly excited about.

Fortunately, I did well in most of the tournaments, so I was able to make more money than I spent and had a fairly successful winter.

Again, it's very difficult! The tour involves a lot of games, with most being 42-game formats en route to the top five. You may bowl great for 41 of those games, and then it comes down to the position round, where you need to bowl another good game to make the top five. One bad break might be the difference between making it and not making it.

You have to combat different lane conditions that sometimes favor your particular kind of roll and sometimes don't. There are just so many different variables, like making the right guesses, because a lot of bowling is educated guesses. You must keep trying to think through what kind of ball you want to throw, what kind of speed, roll, weight distribution, etc., that you want to use. There are so many factors that go into being able to knock all 10 pins down.

There's a lot more to the game of bowling than what you see on television. It looks like the lanes are all the same length and width, with 10 pins, and the balls all the same. It looks like a relatively simple game, but until you really get involved in it on a pro level you don't really understand what goes into it.

THE PROFESSIONAL BOWLING ASSOCIATION

The way some people describe bowling's governing body, the PBA, you might think the organization is working against, not for, bowlers. That's simply not true.

Founded in 1958 by Eddie Elias, the PBA did not take off as most people would imagine, for its first try never got off the ground. But, with the insight and energies of Eddie and some of bowling's greatest players in those days—Dick Weber, Don Carter, Ray Bluth, and others—bowling rolled slowly to its present-day modern version. With the institution of the lane maintenance crew in 1971 and other measures, the PBA moved to change, modify, restructure, and strengthen itself as the need appeared.

An organization is only as good as its people, and for the PBA this is a treasure trove—the PBA has human resources in abundance. The people who run the PBA, from the commissioner all the way down to our tournament directors and press people, are part of a nice organization. The people are friendly.

Our commissioner, Joe Antenora, who doesn't go to a lot of tournaments on a regular basis, does come to quite a few of our winter telecasts, but he's not there from Tuesday to Saturday. He may fly in on a Friday and be there for the telecast to be with the sponsor and the other people who run the tournament. He's a very good administrator and the right person at this time to have in that position.

We have a lot of dedicated people—all the way from the top of the organization right down to everybody else involved. Almost everybody in pro bowling is underpaid to a certain extent, if you make comparisons with other sports. I know our people back at the office work long hard hours, and some people do extensive traveling, putting tournaments together, meeting with the sponsors and the proprietors, and they do exceptional work for us. They work very hard for money that really isn't as good as what that job would dictate, but they still push hard.

Our press people out on tour are a radio and television *press* guide and another gentleman who works with the newspapers and magazines. Their job starts at some time around 9:00 A.M. and goes into the wee hours of the night, especially on a Friday. They'll start fairly early in the morning, and once the top five have been selected, they have to get out all the different releases on all the people in the top five. They may be working till 2:00 or 3:00 in the morning, so they put in a lot of long hard hours. There's a good deal of turnover among our radio, television, and newspaper press people, and whenever somebody leaves I always wonder who will replace him. The PBA always finds somebody who's just fantastic and who's willing to work really hard. I know that Phil Feugerson, our radio and television director for the last couple of years, is just a walking dynamo. His energy level is incredibly high. Phil is a fun guy to be around, even though I can't beat him on the golf course! Our other press man, Johnny Campos, has been with us for a little while and was a very respected newspaperman in San Antonio. He's doing a very good job for us.

Our lane maintenance people, as we discussed before, are in a thankless, pressure cooker job.

HOW TO WATCH A TOURNAMENT

There's an art to everything, and a few tips on how to watch a pro tournament might increase your enjoyment even more. If you have a chance to get to a tournament, by all means do so.

I would pick out just a couple of different bowlers to watch. I'd try to watch a right-hander who throws a lot of hook, and another who throws the ball straight with the same thing on the left-hand side. See how they're bowling and watch to see how accurate they are in relation to their bowling style. If you watch the guys who hook the ball a lot, they're probably a little bit less accurate than the guys who go straight, but does it show on their scores?

The only time I watch bowling is when I watch a telecast. I don't often go in to watch the tournament, but if I'm not in the telecast, I usually watch our Saturday afternoon show because I'm interested in seeing what's happening, who's doing well, whether it's an exciting show with close matches. I watch to see how much area a particular bowler has and whether that area is generated by his release, which can give him extra area on the lane, or by being in the right spot on the lane, or by just knowing where the greatest area is. All bowlers, whether they throw the ball straight or hook in, are trying to generate area because, if you have a spot that is only an inch wide to hit 15–20 feet down the lane, it's more difficult than having a spot 4 inches wide. You're certainly going to be more successful the more area you have.

Also, the more area you have, the looser your swing becomes, and there's definitely a relationship between having a loose swing and knocking 10 pins down. If you're hitting the right spot and your swing is tense, you have a tendency not to strike as much as if you're hitting in a good spot and your swing is loose and fluid. It definitely equates with more stikes.

I do always make it a point to watch the finals. It's an education to store away for future reference, and it gives me clues as to how other bowlers bowl on television under that pressure.

TV FINALS

It all boils down to the last five positions, and after you've made it to the top five on a Friday night, your work is cut out for you, for the next day you will bowl before a national television audience.

When the lights go on, you're in a different world, controlled by time slots, commercials, producers, etc. It is here that your mental game is really tested.

The spectators are now as intense as ever and create a positive electricity in the air. Their eyes are constantly on you, and the only way to prevent this from distracting you is to accept the flow of positive energy and use it to your advantage. You must avoid any distraction they can cause by chattering, coughing, shuffling papers, etc. You must be in your own world. You've come too far to throw it away on something like that, but you'd be surprised how unnerved some bowlers will get.

The camera distracts many a bowler. Just its presence is forbidding and can catch your eye at the most inopportune time.

Concern about doing well can also serve as your undoing, for not being natural will have a negative effect on your game and your ability to withstand pressure.

The experience of having been there before is like money in the bank. It gives you security in knowing what to expect to a reasonable degree so that the surprise's impact will be kept to a minimum. Experience is the best teacher, especially on the telecasts.

What you have to do is very simple. Bowl your game under the most unnatural conditions! Now, isn't that easy? The telecast often separates the physical and the mental game, where the latter is usually the determining factor. Everybody's nervous. Resign yourself to that fact of life. I've been on television more than 60 times, and it still excites me.

Just relax and do your best, incorporating all those things you've learned. It's the closing curtain on your bowling efforts. Have it fall to a "bravo!"; your dedication and sacrifice will pay off with a competitive game you can be proud of.

FUTURE CHANGES IN BOWLING

The changes to come in bowling's future, such as the increased pin weight, will prove that change is a positive element that ensures future growth.

One such change that will have monumental effects on bowling's popularity and growth is participation in the Olympics. I feel this is both inevitable and necessary since bowling is one of the world's largest participation sports and the beauty of international competition will serve the sport of bowling, its fans, and the bowlers. I look forward to this heralded event, for it will release to the world the beauty, drama, suspense, and excitement that is bowling on a scale that knows no boundaries. The result will be a giant step forward for bowling and for the youth of all nations, who will be able to share the joy bowling offers with the people of the world.

8
A FINAL MESSAGE

I guess we've reached the final frame. It's been fun putting down in writing those things that I do instinctively in my game. But before we meet again at the lanes or on television I'd like to share some parting thoughts with you.

The advanced bowler seeking to achieve a competitive game must acknowledge the dedication involved and the practice that is necessary to become a better bowler. It takes more than just natural talent, as we've seen. I know that I never found my natural talent until after many years of hard practice.

It's important that you not limit yourself to working on your game in one facility. You need to move around and slowly graduate into higher competition. You may start from a handicap league, working into scratch leagues and then graduating to local and regional tournaments, with the ultimate goal of making it to national tournaments and possibly to the professional bowlers' tour.

Don't try to complicate the game by trying to concentrate on hand positions, follow-through, etc., while in the middle of an approach—you'll have four or five ideas running wild through your mind. You'll have no chance to do anything. Clear your mind and try to make a clear shot.

Try to simplify the game as much as possible. Even though we've talked about the advanced game, the less technical you can be about it, the freer you will be to let your body do what it knows naturally. I know this is the case for myself and many other pros. We must be free and at ease.

I would recommend that those of you who feel you want to take the shot at the tour do so, if you feel in your heart that you honestly have a shot. I wouldn't recommend going out on the tour as an ultimate way to make a living, because the number of people who go out on the tour and actually succeed is very small. So do it if you have it in your mind, and it's something you really want to pursue.

Don't spend too much time chasing something that may not happen, but give yourself the opportunity and a decent amount of time to try it. This way, you'll be able to say to yourself, "at least I tried it," as opposed to saying, "What if I had . . . ?"

Don't let others discourage you, for often these detractors are motivated by envy or their own unfulfilled dreams. They may simply regret that they never took the chance!

You'd be surprised, once you've made the decision to try, how good it makes you feel, compared to just constantly talking about it.

People need to meet challenges. It teaches them a lot about themselves instead of making them endure a dream world existence.

If you are not seeking to make a career of bowling and wish to improve your game, you must be open-minded about the game and keep in mind that the game of bowling has progressed in the last 10–15 years. It is now at a point where it's similar to golf, because you can't just go in with one particular piece of equipment. You need a variety of equipment. There are different types of balls and other gear that can help you achieve your ultimate goal of knocking more pins down.

But above all, have fun doing what you like. It's important to allow yourself to experience the joy bowling has to offer, be it a competitive game, the enjoyment of playing with fellow workers after a hard day's work, or the romantic experience of a moonlight bowl.

No matter what you pursue in life, do it with a positive, meaningful attitude so your effort will be a rewarding one, even if it doesn't work out.

Remember, give it a shot—the best possible shot you can each and every time—and you will be satisfied with the results, knowing that you've done your very best!

INDEX